WALKING OUR TALK

A JOURNEY THROUGH THE MAZE OF CROSS-RACE FRIENDSHIP

KARI BOWER AND La FONDA RIGGINS

ISBN-13:
978-1532829512
ISBN-10:
1532829515

2

TABLE OF CONTENTS

Introduction

For twenty years we have been friends, one black, one white. We aren't the type of friends that say, "Have a nice weekend" on Friday, then greet each other with "How was your weekend?" on Monday. We are the kind that say; "What should I say to my husband about his behavior?" or "Can I interview for another job without telling anyone?" on Friday, then greet each other on Monday with "Tell me everything!" For twenty years we have shared the births, deaths, divorces, disappointments and successes of our lives. For twenty years, we have ribbed each other about being the only person at each other's social gatherings from another racial group. "So am I gonna be an only at this party?" is how we phrase it. "What should I bring? What should I wear?" is our code for "I don't want to look completely clueless around your people; help me out a bit." It's a joke now. We call ourselves the "only's" as in "Nice to meet you, I am Kari's only tonight." Usually people are surprised by the introduction but it's proved a decent ice-breaker none the less. We laugh about the awkward situations we have encountered at each other's celebrations. There was the time when La Fonda wouldn't enter the kitchen at Kari's party.

She poked her head in the kitchen door, told Kari, "I can't come in here girl, you know everyone will think I'm the maid!" We get a good laugh about the birthday lunch where Kari was the only white person at our table of eight and wasn't served her entre until everyone else had desert. We asked for the food a few times; the reply didn't change, "Coming right out"

Is this stuff funny? What does it mean? Are we the only cross-race friends talking about these encounters with each other? Are these friendships as rare as they seem? We have always felt that our tales of two friends, hanging out in one city, have enhanced our lives. Some of these experiences have caused us to say to one another, "We ought to write this shit down!" As with so many things friends dream about over a glass of wine, we never seemed to find the time or energy; then fate jumped in. We were offered a job that required us to spend ten full days together as we worked on developing, writing and delivering a training program for staff at a residential recovery facility. The residence housed women and their children up to age three. Our training was supposed to help the staff best advise these women on successful parenting while also practicing cultural sensitivity. The task required lots of talking, collaborating and writing.

Our half joking daydreams returned. Surely if we can do this, we could tell our own stories, was how we began convincing each other. Why not? It could be interesting, even fun, to share these experiences with people beyond our immediate circle. Maybe we could increase understanding between people that rarely interact. Our conversations progressed. We decided it would be helpful to engage in future experiences with a more deliberately focused attention on our settings and our interactions. We would become amateur anthropologists going to all sorts of venues together while focusing on our internal perceptions of the comfort or discomfort we felt. Before letting these feeling pass unnoticed or be forgotten, we would take mental, and actual, notes to discuss and compare. We made lists of potential outings. "How about movie theaters, restaurants and open houses for sale in different parts of town?" We could venture into all sorts of ethnic neighborhoods going into Grocery stores and nail salons. We ought to see films and read books on the subject of cross-cultural interaction." Our brainstorms became exciting.

Actually, our first outing was on the calendar anyway. Kari was set to attend a surprise birthday party for La Fonda planned by her teenage son, Morgan. She is the only white person at the party, but doesn't feel out of place. Watching and listening diligently on that day didn't seem to produce any remarkable moments to file away for future discussion. Does this feeling of familiarity and belonging occur because Kari is an old friend of Fonda's? We felt sort of "deflated" that we weren't handed any of those awkward "race moments" to talk about now that we were trying to put them to paper. After some thought, we concluded that the surprise dinner at Fonda's mom house that night WAS a story! It was a story that is rare in this socially segregated world of ours. It was a story of the comfort and acceptance that exposure and interaction can achieve with enough time and effort. Morgan was seventeen now. It wasn't always so comfortable to be the only!

For Morgan's second birthday, Kari attended the first of many celebrations hosted by La Fonda. This one was a bar-b-queue at beautiful park on your typical sunny Los Angeles day. Kari bent down, lifted her sunglasses and greeted a little black girl of about four. The way Kari tells it, that the child screamed as those glasses came up. The freckle faced, blue-eyed devil was here in the flesh! Fonda swore then, and maintains now, that the child was afraid of sunglasses and not white people. I wasn't buying it. We disagreed.

At first it was awkward, and then it was funny! It was the catalyst for the kind of face to face "race talk" that can move people forward in conversation, and ultimately in trust. Unfortunately, these talks don't happen enough in our communities, if at all.

The two of us committed to continue with our exploration. We would start with places where we didn't know anyone, places where we might feel different or uncomfortable, Places where we might bare witness to the subtle acts of bias that keep people apart and uncomfortable. We would go forward keeping the words of the renowned African American author, professor and activist, Cornel West, in our heads and hearts. He asks three things of us: "Be curious, start with empathy, give testimony."

Not a week later the world heard about the verdict in Ferguson, Missouri. A white police officer is acquitted of all charges after shooting an unarmed black teenager nine times until he died. Fonda says "Race is everything" Kari wants to question the statement. It wasn't the right time. We agreed that cameras on police officers might have helped Mike Brown get justice. "Cops should wear cameras," the experts tell us. "It will make a big difference."

Another week passes; another white officer is acquitted of killing an unarmed black man. However, this time there was a camera, the camera of an unnoticed civilian bystander. This time, the policeman was attempting to arrest a man for selling single cigarettes on a street corner in New York. The man engaging in this arrest able New York crime, had the temerity to question the officer as to why such a harsh punishment for selling single cigarettes. The response to an unarmed and lucid Eric Garner for daring to open his mouth in protest, was immediate. The white officer choked the man, pulled him to the cement and squeezed the breath out of him with the help of four other NYPD in the middle of the afternoon on a sidewalk. The camera didn't make a difference. "I can't believe this!" said the shocked white friend. "You better believe it!" said her black friend. For the first time in a long time, many other shocked white people were forced to believe it too!

This is a systematic problem. It's the police, Government, education, prison and more.

What is the significance of our little friendship story as we watch Eric Garner die over and over on television saying "I can't breathe" as four uniformed and armed men sworn "to protect and to serve", suffocate him? Maybe our book is pointless. The white girl says she needs to learn more. She needs to read more. She needs to watch more PBS; no getting snacks during commercials on the news-bite channels; watch real news. Watch for a WHOLE hour! She did.

After just one night of following this plan, the PBS news hour broadcast an interview with an African American poet and professor. It lasted for fifteen minutes. No sound bites, just sentences. The poet was a finalist for the national poetry book

9

award and her book is titled "Citizen" Her name is Claudia
Rankine. Her book is about what she calls micro-aggressions.
These are the every day situations of unkindness, ignorance and
invisibility many people of color live with. She also speaks of
the indignities people of low income and low status from all
ethnic groups often endure. She teaches that these many micro-
aggressions are closely related to the major aggressions that
result in the killing of men like Eric Garner. She states that
these daily uncomfortable insults must be understood in order
for all of us to see the larger picture. Dr. Rankine, thank
you! Maybe our little story does matter. Following is a poem
from her book describing the sort of micro-aggression many
university students and faculty of color encounter daily:

*You are in the dark, in the car, watching the black-tarred
street being swallowed by speed; he tells you his dean is
making him hire a person of color when there are so many
great writers out there.*
*You think maybe this is an experiment and you are being
tested or retroactively insulted or you have done something
that communicates this is an okay conversation to be having.
Why do you feel okay saying this to me? You wish the light
would turn red or a police siren would go off so you could
slam on the brakes, slam into the car ahead of you, be
propelled forward so quickly both your faces would suddenly
be exposed to the wind.*
*As usual you drive straight through the moment with the
expected backing off of what was previously said. It is not
only that confrontation is headache producing; it is also
that you have a destination that doesn't include acting like
this moment isn't inhabitable, hasn't happened before, and
the before isn't part of the now as the night darkens and the
time shortens between where we are and where we are going.*
*When you arrive in your driveway and turn off the car, you
remain behind the wheel another ten minutes. You fear the
night is being locked in and coded on a cellular level and*

can this work both ways? Can I be totally nauseated by my white affluent friends? Ignore them? is nore not ignore, No responsibilty away?

want time to function as a power wash. Sitting there staring at the closed garage door you are reminded that a friend once told you there exists a medical term —John Henryism— for people exposed to stresses stemming from racism. They achieve themselves to death trying to dodge the build up of erasure. Sherman James, the researcher who came up with the term, claimed the physiological costs were high. You hope by sitting in silence you are bucking the trend.

Rankine provides the reader with a taste of the daily micro-aggressions piercing the souls of weary recipients every day. These are the painful and invisible pinpricks not seen on TV. Micro-aggressions are the startling jabs that keep some feeling less-than, angry and vigilantly alert to the next "stab". Over time, we learn to stay away from others who might offend; we chose to avoid the stresses when possible by following the advice of the woman sitting silently in her garage. We try to "buck the trend." We gravitate toward a comfort zone filled with predictable conversation and style.

This discomfort is one of many factors contributing to our segregation from the stranger in the room. The two of us chose a different path. We listened to Dr. Cornell West, revered activist, and Princeton professor, deliver these lines to a Diversity Inc. conference, and knew our choice was correct.

"I am still wrestling with the white supremist inside of me after 59 years. It is easier to live in the bubble, keep a critical distance from examining those racist, sexist and homophobic impulses inside of us. I need to be with others who will engage in Socratic dialogue and critique of me with the idea of encouraging and empowering me. Only when engaging as human to human, soul to soul, face to face, eye to eye, can your empathetic juices begin flowing."

The goal is empathy! It is not agreement. Meaningful examination of our choices brings curiosity about the choices of others. Curiosity gets us face to face. It gives us a name. It moves us forward. It gets us talking. For these two women it creates the trust that allows us to speak honestly about the micro-aggressions individually experienced and the macro-aggressions felt by the less powerful in our shared community. This understanding helps us empower each other. It creates friendship. We hope our story helps others to create the same. Lets take it to the streets.

What Kari taught me about me

We decided to name the chapter we penned alone, about each other, with the same title. We talked about the question. I thought about Kari as a trusted friend. I have stories to back up the assumption. She has a great way of listening without making judgmental remarks, but I wasn't so clear on what she taught me about *me.* She tried to help. "What is the first thing you remember about me", she asked. I let her know it was when she got all upset in the office because the tree she ordered for her yard was too small, cost $300, and she just didn't have ten years to sit around waiting for some stick to grow into a tree. I remember thinking "This girl is worried her new tree is too small and I struggle with paying regular household bills; what could we possibly have in common?" "Well, that's fucking great!" was her reply. "Your first memory of me was that I was a spoiled brat who you didn't much like?" She pressed on…"How about something else, something you remember once we became friendly?" I told her I remember she asked me why I hardly ever smiled and that I really thought about that comment; I knew it was a stereotype whites often applied to black women and in my heart I knew that her observation twenty years ago was right.

During that time I was experiencing a great deal of personal and financial stress. I worked weekends at a "secret" second job at Target and was too embarrassed to let anyone know. I was so caught up trying to avoid being viewed by others, or feeling myself, to be the stereotype of the single black mother, that I allowed little joy into my life. I was neglecting my authentic self and what I had achieved by focusing on this cloud of temporary disappointment. Kari was the one who reminded me that being divorced doesn't take away from being a college educated, employed, home owning, loving and responsible black mother.

That remark of her's, the one about the smile, had me wondering how others in my office viewed me? I did have a lot to deal with, yes. But I was also lucky to be inhabiting that office with a rare group of co-workers for us black folks, an incredibly diverse bunch coming from nearly every ethnic, gender, and sexual orientation group on the map; why not take a risk and let these folks into my life a little bit! I took a risk; I decided to reveal more, talk more, and smile more around the office. It turned out that in that office, shared

with Kari and a rainbow of others, was the most fun work
experience I have ever had, and more than that, was the place
where I made the best friendships of my life!

Maybe her question has some relevance after all. I suppose
there have been a few times Kari Sue taught me a thing or two
about me. For instance, I learned that I spent way too much
energy worrying about my status in the hierarchy of too many
situations and too many conversations in the moment I was
having them, then wasted additional energy wondering what
others thought of *me after I returned home*. The energy I used
up comparing and measuring was definitely a drain on my joy
and scraped away at what should have been a sense of well-
earned confidence.

Smiling doesn't have to mean softness

When Kari commented on my lack of smile, she spoke from a
place of concern and interest. I have no doubt that plenty of
white people who ask plenty of black people in their
peripheral lives why they aren't smiling, are also asking out
of concern. Most whites, especially white women, are part of
a cultural group, the dominant one in America, that values
lots of smiling, because for them, freely smiling at just
about anybody signifies acceptance and welcoming. What most
of our white majority culture doesn't know, is that during
slavery, during Jim crow, and often since, black folks were

required to display a sweet easy smile around white

people. This was a way for my people to show employers and

others in authority that they shouldn't be feared. A freely

given smile likely represents weakness or servitude in my

subconscious sense memory.

For me, to smile at a stranger could invite lots of prying

questions and feel like an invasion of my privacy. The

carefree and open smile may not come as naturally in my

culture as in yours; this does not mean I am angry! It does

mean that for all of us human beings, cultural norms are

learned and practiced from the time we are children. The

advantage definitely goes to those who are in the majority

and are able to dictate the "norms" of any given cultural

setting. For those of us for whom a particular cultural

behavior is new or uncomfortable, it may take a while to

adapt to majority behavioral expectations when necessary; we

might go as far as choosing to *adopt*--a more willing and

comfortable choice than to *adapt*--if it feels right!

Research is clear that the stereotype of the "angry,

unapproachable black woman" is very much alive in most

majority white employee, and majority white student, settings

in which we occupy common space. It seems unfair to me that I

remain constantly aware of my facial expression, the tone of

my voice, and the delivery of my opinion, when I am simply

trying to do *MY WORK!* I found it distressing to read the following quote in an August, 2015 Essence magazine article given to a journalist by a black female design executive when asked about her experience with racism as a skilled professional living and working in London:

"The interesting thing about it here is that often times racism can be so covert that you sometimes wonder if it actually happened or if you're overreacting. I've experienced countless micro-aggressions, especially at work. Once a colleague was convinced that each time we spoke I came off aggressively, and even said she was afraid I was going to "do something" to her. This went on for three weeks before I raised the issue with my boss. Needless to say, trying to explain a micro-aggression to someone who has never experienced one was a challenge."

I see this extra layer of awareness is not only a necessity in America! Of course, the need to "go along to get along" is not the worst thing a person could deal with in this life. I could focus on reframing the "Its not fair" message bouncing around in my head into one that tells me; "I am increasing my knowledge of, and ability to, navigate cultural difference without loosing myself; that's a positive!

However, I would be more inclined to adopt my new message if more people operating from the majority "cultural norm" would wonder a bit more about the *"why"* of another's different conversational style, facial expression, or comfort with the amount of physical space than is typically comfortable for them. I ask for your willingness to increase your cultural knowledge, not only because I want to be better

17

understood and accepted, but also because I cannot be expected to make you "feel better" anytime you think I am "not nice, too sensitive or racist against white people." Before demanding that I agree with your indignant claim; "YOU KNOW I DON'T HAVE A RACIST BONE IN MY BODY!" Ask yourself if there exists a "Why" for the reaction that doesn't make sense to you and then be sure to take a moment and give additional thought to the "why" of your reaction.

I remember long ago seeing an explanation for the reason black folks may seem "overly sensitive" or "overly suspicious" toward white folks; it resonated with me. The writer, who's name I unfortunately have forgotten, asked that we imagine a great many blacks in America walk around wearing invisible long sleeve shirts to cover up years of large painful bruises. The bruises are not easily seen, but when touched are still tender. I admit to being in situations in which I reacted to small slaps as if they were delivered with a giant stick; it wouldn't hurt to work on my skill at differentiating another's slap from a bloody blow.

For instance, I recently attended an event and saw some black folks across the room. It was nice to sit down and share a business lunch with a group of "my people" for a change. A white coworker with whom I get along, approached me at the buffet and said with a little chuckle, "I see you are sitting at the BROTHAH table; I guess we aren't good enough for you; what if I made a white table?" I told her in my best low, direct, and unmistakably angry voice, "I don't give a damn who you sit with!" She looked at me with one of those typical wide-eyed "Don't get upset with me, I'm just an innocent white girl" kind of looks and then blurted out, as expected, "You know I didn't mean anything by it!" In retrospect, it *was* a slap, one of a series of slaps that I had let bubble up inside and stress me out until this particular slap morphed into a baseball bat sized blow. Maybe this is the result of a cultural message telling me to stay composed, feel fortunate to have this position, show em' how "classy" you are. The problem is that in allowing all the little slaps to take up space in *my* head, *my* heart and *my* stomach, *my* mental health and career are negatively affected! The "angry black woman" persona was historically meant to protect, but does have a downside.

Finally, there is another widely held stereotype used to describe the successful, strong and accomplished in the black community. This one doesn't initially feel so "damning" as the "Angry" one; it's the "strong and invincible" black woman label. It's the one that elicits comments like "You are incredible, you have the responsibilities of two or three "average" people! How is it possible to have a job, take your kids to all those activities, volunteer for the school and cook meals every day? You are superhuman!" Mellissa Harris Perry calls this "the strong black woman soldier" in her book "Shame Stereotypes and Black Women in America". This label describes me far more accurately than the "angry" one does. Oh yeah, the complements given to this *strong soldier woman* are abundant, but so too are the expectations! Harris Perry passionately describes the enormous weight placed on these "extra special" sisters of mine:

"If you are weak or sad or need help, you are not meeting the expectations of your community or of the American community."

As she reads these words aloud for me on YouTube, clapping her hands loudly and quickly as if demonstrating just how in step and non-stop this super black woman is supposed to be. I listen to her, transfixed by her knowledge of the weariness and frustration, never said out loud, born by the financially stable, educated and skilled single black mothers everywhere. Our task, assigned by our community, is to project only pride and fulfillment to the scrutinizing eyes of the world.

Listening to, or reading the words of, other successful black women, is a great way to get some virtual "coaching" and inspiration. For example, a quick trip around the web introduced me to Sandra Miles, Ph.D. Director of the office of student affairs at Indiana University-Purdue University Columbus. She delivered this no-nonsense advice to the group

attending her lecture called: "I don't go to work to make
friends", during the March 2013 NASPA conference:

"Yes, racism and sexism are unjust. Yes, white privilege and
male privilege are problems. That doesn't require us to let
that rock keep rolling down the hill again and again like
Sisyphus until equity is achieved. To advance professionally
is not abandoning the larger cause but gaining more power to
do something about it. "So what are we going to do, ladies?"
Miles asked. "I speak as someone who did it wrong for many
years. Those who could promote me had no clue as to who I
am." To have them think of you at promotion time, do the
things that others on campus are already doing. Connect with
others and not just your friends."

She continued with suggestions for specific strategies:

• Be more personal and personable. Be genuine in a positive
way you're comfortable with. Don't complain about being tired
or busy or underpaid; save that for your real friends. You
want to be a person that people want to be around. You can do
this without changing your work habits or core personality
traits.

• Get to know your colleagues. "How was your weekend?"
"Great, how was yours?" Until you know each other, you don't
know whom you can trust and they don't know whether they can
trust you. Miles attended regular meetings where the
conversation before it revolved around getting drunk. She
finally joined the banter, saying, "Look, I draw the line on
moonshine." After that remark, others felt that they could
trust her.

• Attend gatherings at co-workers' homes when invited. A
white woman repeatedly invited Miles to come have wine on her
porch. When she finally did, the woman was delighted and
started inviting others to come meet her.

• Have gatherings at your home and invite co-workers. Be
willing to take the initiative. If you wait to be asked, you
may wait a long time.

. Stop assuming hard work will get you noticed. If you want
to get promoted, you need to be the one getting noticed, for
the right reasons.

Ironically, Dr. Miles has the word smile in her E-mail address. Is this choice connected to the Angry Black Woman stereotype? I have no idea, but it did get me thinking! Studies report that in America smiling in the workplace is widely read as a signal of ones approachability and confidence—both advantages for the ambitious among us. In addition, I uncovered fascinating research claiming that when we smile, our bodies produce increased amounts of the hormone associated with immunity building and of those associated with the feeling of mental well being; these hormones actually decrease when we frown.

Sometimes I got to represent

Every African American person I know, every kid, every adult, every woman and every man, can tell familiar tales of the annoying and exhausting right of passage for any of us who spend a certain amount of time around white people; it's called "having to represent" For those who don't know, representing is a term that means being asked to answer all sorts of questions pertaining to the ways of black folks. I could be asked to answer on behalf of my black self, on behalf of my black hair, on behalf of my black child, on behalf of other black women or on behalf of all black people in the United States of America. There are countless websites and print pages filled with the most common and offending of the "questions"; In fact, there is an entire Ivy league college hash-tag campaign called "I too am Harvard" and "I too am Princeton" showing nothing but African American college students on video explaining why "Is that a weave", or "You are lucky to black so you can get into Harvard", are insulting and racist! Remember, these are comments coming from other members of the "best and brightest" that are supposed to be populating these pinnacle campuses.

Actually, many of the same words spoken to the students at Harvard are also the words said to the woman in the grocery, the kid in the classroom, the guy in the office and to the "friend" at the party.

Some are so ridiculous that they leave me feeling more confused and dumbstruck than angry. These routinely include:

"Can you teach me how to dance like a black girl?"

"What is a forty?"

"Do you live in the ghetto?"

"I don't think of you as black"

"Can you bring some soul food to the office for me to try?"

"You are so lucky your son isn't in a gang!"

"Can I touch your hair?"

"What position does your son play in basketball?"

"Why do black people go to churches where people cry and scream?"

"Why have a Black Entertainment Channel and not a White Entertainment Channel on television?"

"Did you love the movie *Twelve Years a Slave*?"

"How can I be a racist if I have black friends?"

However, there are other questions asked and statements made regularly by white folks, that are considered quite hurtful and insulting to most of the Black people I know. Common phrases in this particular category include:

"How did you get this… job, acceptance letter, invitation, car, house?"

"You are so articulate!"

"I don't think a police officer would stop a person for no reason at all. They must have done something"

"If they didn't do anything wrong they wouldn't have be worried about being followed by a store owner or walking down the street in a majority White neighborhood."

"Why would we have a black president if racism still exists?"

"How am I supposed to understand racism if you won't take the time to explain it to me?"

"Why do the black people always sit together and don't want to mix with us?"

I know I mentioned earlier that this "*Representing*" thing could be annoying and exhausting for those of us given the task. I am mentioning it again, and with good reason! Sometimes our decades old, and tender bruises are poked in such a way that they seem to rip wide open. When it happens, you may hear my pain cry out with what you believe to be a shocking over-reaction with "Why the hell would you say that to me?" or the equally unsettling icy silence. Believe it or not, as a result of working on this book, I do see there were occasions in which I overreacted to a comment made by a white person who spoke out of ignorance and was, I believe, lacking bad intention. Actually, the research I have done while reading and listening to the words of other black folks has convinced me that some members of my community also "over-react" now and again. I remember two of these in particular. Both stories left me with a desire to "turn back the clock" and find a way to change the outcomes to the benefit of all involved.

The first appeared in an essay by Emily Bernard in her book, "Some of My Best Friends" She told of a relationship she once had with a white woman, Susan. She described herself as being "besotted" with this woman with whom she "shared uncanny similarities and felt completely understood" until a question from Susan that Bernard said "changed everything" Susan asked Emily "What does the black community really think about names like Sheniqua and Tyronda, because the white community thinks they are just bizarre." At that moment the author describes feeling herself "turned in the eyes of her love into the black community instead of being seen as an individual woman with whom she shared so much." Emily tried to cover her bruise, just now carelessly slapped and in such an unexpected and painful way. The reader learns this particular bruise didn't heal, and that the author believes her silence during the next two years is partly to blame. I felt Emily's reaction to Susan created an unnecessary loss of friendship as well as the loss of an opportunity to "represent" during an instance when it was probably worth the extra effort. I asked Kari what she thought about the essay. Her answer, in a typical funny, flippant, Kari style, came without hesitation: "When someone asks you that question, why not ask the offender what the white community thinks about names like Brittany, Brandi, Mellissa and Ethan, because *some* in your community think *they* are bizarre!" I actually think the reply makes a strong and serious point minus the "heaviness" of a tense "I am not my community" talk.

Another memorable tale of relationship ending racial tension which left me wishing for a real life rewind button, is the one shared by a guy attending one of our workshops. He wasn't a teacher, so had no mandate or financial incentive for attending a continuing education class. He said he sought out our class so that he might better understand how what he had considered a mundane conversation with a student at a youth leadership retreat, became the catalyst for him being accused of racism and getting fired from his job as a youth counselor. He shared his version of what happened with our class:

"I asked a black kid standing next to me in the food line which position he played in basketball. I didn't mean to offend him. I was trying to make small talk and he was wearing gym shorts. He didn't reply but I guess he later complained to a director that I had assumed he played basketball because he was black, and felt the question was offensive and racist."

During this "confession", John's face and voice filled with obvious anger and dismay. He described the organization he worked for as portraying itself as a place of extraordinary caring, empathy, non-judgment and open-minded liberal values. SURPRISE: A sarcastic eye-roll accompanied the syrupy description of his former employer! Guess who will clam up or walk away the next time he encounters difference? You got it!

Now, I know the "Do you play basketball?" question is an offensive one for many black folks; I also agree that there is good reason to find the question offensive. However, I imagine few white people understand *why* the assumption is offensive; it offends because of a long held stereotype that black men are "brawn without brains", and playing basketball is the only way they can achieve success academically or financially. In my opinion, and in this instance, John deserved a decent explanation as to why he had insulted the student as well as an opportunity to make a sincere and informed apology to the young man. In my opinion there are times when the tired old comment, "Oh my, I certainly didn't mean to offend you!" is more than a slippery attempt to escape responsibility, wriggle away from the "overly sensitive" black person, and adjust the giant "innocent victim" crown on your head. Sometimes the words are truly sincere, coming from a place of interest in doing the right thing coupled with a desire to become a more culturally competent person. In these instances, even the weary and cynical among us could choose to step-up and "represent"!

You may prefer instead to retreat to a familiar corner of comfort and acceptance wondering why the ignorant can't just open a book or tap on Google for information about your people. Believe me, I have wondered the same! However, all in all, the extra effort I put into patiently answering and explaining when appropriate, has been a positive experience; that is, as long as I continue to maintain the ability to wisely choose who or what is worth my time and effort, and who or what is not worth it!

I do believe I laid out a decent argument as to why "representing" within limits is a good idea for creating more comfort and career advancement in the workplace for people in the minority, and also a good idea for reducing the sort of stress that tends to shadow us home after having one of those tense and unaddressed culture based encounters. I have another reason, and it's simply numeric logic. The fact is there just aren't enough black folks around! We are only about 13% of the U.S. population. Although, our numbers of college graduates, white-collar professionals and elected officials have grown near 500% in the past forty years; we comprise a small segment of *all* members of these categories. Had you seen the enormous amount of coverage given the results of a 2013 PRRI study disclosing that African Americans report having eight white friends for every one black friend a typical white person reports having, you would have thought we are more than 13% of the U.S. population.

The white/black friend statistics became a "hot topic" all over the "astonished" blogosphere with posts like:

"If 75% of white people have no black friends" asked one particularly astute writer, "How can they all be claiming the "some of my best friends are black" excuse as proof of their NON-RACIST credentials? Amen!

I certainly don't want to give the impression that numbers are the only reason for a lack of meaningful interaction between our groups, but I am surprised that this fact was rarely mentioned in the many articles and broadcasts focused solely on our mutual state of segregated living, schooling and socializing as the main culprit. You see, knowing our number may be a catalyst for nudging members of my community to more often consider speaking up and "representing" for the brothers and sisters that don't have the chance.

For me, the best reason for taking on the burden of "*representing*" is to become one of the souls who helps remove some small bits of the obstacles still blocking the path traveled by my son and others like him. In fact, this belief once propelled me to offer unsolicited "representing" advice to a person of authority before thinking of the possible consequence of such a bold move; I humbly believe it changed both of us for the better! My unsolicited advice cleared an obstacle from the interior path of another city employee of color that day. This person, my superior, was one of the few high rank officers of color in the county.

The day marked the first time he came by our station. I noticed the rank and file officers seemed very chummy and friendly with him—- showing none of the stoic deference generally given white superiors who visited. I later discovered I was the only one who was aware of his rank. When the others learned of it, the apologies flowed! He was greeted with the proper amount of deference and respect from then on. I wonder if it simply didn't feel "natural" or "normal" for white men to think of a black man as their superior at first glance.

After the initial meeting, all the guys asked him to pose for pictures when he came to the station. Many officers wanted to pose for pictures alone with him in addition to assembling group shots. The official looked hesitant and uncomfortable with the requests. Based on my own experience being "the black face" in photos and on the feelings expressed to me by friends in this situation over the years, I assumed he felt like a sort of representative token in these pictures. I decided to pull the big boss aside, sucked in my breath and in the most confidant voice I could muster, told him he was not taking these photos for himself, but was taking them for his son and grandson. Well, not only did the chief stand for the requested photos; he began sitting front and center every chance he got! I know I changed his perception in that moment and will never forget the "ahhah" look on his face as he accepted my advice to "represent" for his grandson no matter how it felt to him.

I was already comfortable "representing" in pictures. However, it was still awkward and uncomfortable to take on the challenge of *representing* during risky and uncomfortable conversations I tended to avoid in the past. Maybe my words could end up paving a smoother path for my son and his interactions down the road.

It stunned even me the first time I decided to answer, rather than avoid or dance around, my white republican supervisor's question; "What do you think about Ferguson?" "Here we go", I thought. "We are about to enter the most divided racial territory imaginable, views about the actions of police." I started by saying, "I just feel so sad that an 18 year old is dead." He replied, "I agree", and then remained quiet waiting for me to speak. I knew at that moment I could have a "race talk" with this man. I knew he was seeking knowledge and understanding from talking about this with me. I could speak to him without being hit with a series of "but what about…" and "race wasn't part of it" declarations. I'm glad I opened up to him and felt heard.

Kari is always pestering me for an answer to the *"why"* of culture based differences she observes or hears regarding members of my community. Sometimes I get tired of all the *"representing"* she requires and just want to get back to laughing about our escapades!

It's usually *"all good"* until I slip up and look at her crossways for doing or saying something *"weird"* in what I consider to be a stereotypically white style. For example, I can't help shooting her the "look" when she casually mentions that her neighbor held a funeral for her dog and paid a guy to cast the dog's paw prints in plaster and frame them in gold. "Why is that weird?" she wants to know. "Why don't black people love dogs or petting zoo's anyway? Is it because of germs?" I explain my take on the subject: "In my community, dogs tend to be around to protect property. They are dirty and shouldn't bring their dirt and fleas onto your child's bed. Now, what's crazy about that?" Usually that's enough and we move on. This past year we were working in a rough neighborhood with loose dogs all over the place. My white friend was in such a state when she spied a chi-Wawa dart into the street, that she literally screamed and slammed her eyes shut while driving into a busy intersection in fear that she would see the dog crushed!

Somehow, seeing that vision brought "why's" out of me that had not surfaced in years! I gave my friend an earful! "You are gonna kill us for a god damn dog. White people are so worried about sick dogs; they ought to worry more about dead black boys! Michael Vick spent more time in jail for killing a couple of dogs than most people who kill a black kid in cold blood will ever spend in jail. Do you ever ask why everyone freaked out when Tiger Woods cheated on his "good decent" white wife, but it's not big news when a white guy cheats on his wife? She answered me; "That's interesting Fonda, I never thought about it like that." No doubt, this "representing" thing surely involves some educating.

More Authentic exposure has brought me more authentic composure

Isn't it assumed that a member of the black middle class in America gets loads of exposure to our country's majority white middle class while crossing paths in the corporate, educational and social settings we share? Isn't typical white middle class culture considered the default norm for the rest of us? Haven't members of my community been schooled by family and mentors as to the need to do ten times more to get the same as "them"? When one of us peaks into the classroom of a private "elite" school or walks the corridors of a successful business, don't we expect to see so few black folks that we half joke to friends; "It looks like seeing flies in buttermilk?" "Come on," you say to yourself, "Why on earth would I need *more* exposure? If anything, I am *over-exposed*!" I would say that you are technically correct, but that the word that matters most in my heading for this section is the word authentic!

I, and so many of my educated, employed, and accomplished African American cohorts, have heard about the added hurdles we face and the extra tenacity we need, to overcome this thing called "white privilege". Unfortunately, in my opinion, we don't fully trust in the far-reaching existence of that privilege. I say this because, if we as a group understood white privilege to be as factual and pervasive as it is, then we wouldn't be reading the following story told to Claude Steele, Ph.D. by a friend in higher education, and retold in his book "Whistling Vivaldi"; a book which examines the effect of life long messages about our behavior, worth and status from those around us, on the development of our cultural identity and sense of self in the world:

"Carol Porter, a social psychologist who has devoted herself to bettering the undergraduate experience at places like Princeton and Yale, mentioned offhandedly something she noticed while advising students in organic chemistry. She told me the African American students approached the course differently than the white or Asian students; that the white and Asian students would often take the course once for no grade before taking it a second time for a grade, or would take chemistry over the summer at a less competitive school. But when these strategies were suggested to the African American students, they often rejected it, studying in isolation and then loosing the chance to drop the class before grades were reported. This was the gateway course for getting into med school and she didn't know why the black kids on campus refused to pursue the easier route taken by their white and Asian peers."

This was not the first time Steele heard this story from university colleagues. Actually, there is a name for the phenomenon, "over-efforting". This is when students of color become so invested in disproving the stereotype hanging over their heads and recalling parental whispers to "work ten times harder"; it can end up harming their future!

I am convinced that this "over-efforting" thing is a result of either not believing, or not knowing, the way things are done in the privileged world. The best way to get the "skinny" is to get some authentic exposure, the kind I get from friends like Kari; she likes to call it "opening the white files". She says in her world, it is perfectly acceptable dinner conversation to ask anybody at the table if they "have an in" to gain admission to a school or know someone who might "make a call" in order to get a job or internship. I was surprised to hear that a relative "made a call" to get her mother moved up three months on a surgery list. She also tells me that just about anything one of her people can't ask for they can buy.

It's common knowledge to folks in my community, that a school described as "good", is probably mostly white. However, what I didn't know, according to Kari, is the amount spent by parents like her on supplementary tutors, classes and therapy that go along with these "good" schools. It runs into hundreds per month. "Not to mention", she boasts, "by volunteering in the class one day per week, helping with some fundraising activities and giving about $300 to my kids school, I was treated like a queen!" She quickly adds, "That's only for the public school years; I imagine any special treatment to be had at private school costs quite a bit more than $300! Sounds like this benefit is only available to parents with extra time, money and the confidence to march into the school and "stake their claim"

According to her, typical white parents also tell their kids they should be comfortable asking their teachers any question at any time, including at lunch break or after school. My friend says all the white kids she knows hear this message from kindergarten on: "The teachers are there to serve you; asking for help is not ever a sign of stupidity nor an imposition. I do wish more black students felt that same sense of entitlement; my experience tells me we don't. I read a book, *"The Short Tragic Life of Robert Peace"*, in which the author vividly and heartbreakingly describes the downside of this unwillingness on the part of students of color to seek help when enrolled at elite Ivy league Yale University; an unwillingness none of the white or asian students on campus seemed to be experiencing:

"Yale has an infrastructure in place geared toward students whose upbringings haven't necessarily prepared them for college life. There are counselors, advisors and tutors readily available and free. But the kids most likely to use these resources, need them the least: the Exeter grads, the future Rhodes scholars, the affluent students, who from the day they were born were primed to believe adults exist almost exclusively to help them."

And just so you know this *"white files"* thing isn't simply hearsay from a friend, consider the following data collected for a study of white attitudes about race for her book, *"The American non dilemma: Race Inequality Without Racism"*, by sociologist Nancy Ditomaso:

"The vast majority of white respondents assumed everyone has the same opportunities, and they just somehow tried harder, were smarter; not seeing or acknowledging how whites help other whites as a primary way inequality gets reproduced today is helpful. It's easier on the mind. "So white Americans tell a neighbor's son about a job, hire a friend's daughter or carry the resume of a friend's boyfriend's sister into the boss's office. But since most Americans, white and black, live virtually segregated lives, and since advantages, privileges and economic progress have already accrued in favor of whites, the advantages that flow from this sort of help go almost exclusively to whites."

Let me get this straight; White folks are not only brought up to believe that an "all access pass" is a birthright not a privilege, available to those who put forth the effort, but that the *exact* same access is available to anyone from any background who is willing to work hard.

I trust that the sense of composure I mentioned at the start of this essay is the result of my fully embracing the value of my life's experience. For me, it's the knowledge that I have come further with less, than most of my white peers. I recognize there is an impactful difference between a child hearing the message, "You got to fight for it, you got to do better to be noticed" and the message, "You deserve everything you want and the adults in your life are here to help you get it!" I see a middle ground for my son. He should never, for even a moment, have the degrading feeling that he "doesn't belong here" because he doubts his value, nor should he naively skip around in a fog of invincibility and loose his strength. I was moved to tears reading this excerpt from the book, "Between the world and me", penned by Ta Nehisi Coates as a love letter to his son. For me, his words flawlessly explain the nobility in possessing an inner confidence expertly fused with sharp realism.

"The fact is that despite their dreams, their lives are also not inviolable. When their own vulnerability becomes real—when the police decide that tactics intended for the ghetto should enjoy wider usage, when their armed society shoots down their children, when nature sends hurricanes against their cities—they are shocked by the rages of logic and the natural world in a way that those of us who were born and bred to understand cause and effect can never be. And I would not have you live like them. You have been cast into a race in which the wind is always at your face and the hounds are always at your heels. And to varying degrees this is true of all life. The difference is that you do not have the privilege of living in ignorance of this essential fact."

What Fonda taught me about me

The title of this chapter says it all. Generally, when we think about people that teach us something, we think about getting new information. When I think about the teaching I get from Fonda and others like her, I think about using that information to enhance my perceptions and interactions. It is the kind of learning that helps me understand that long held assumptions that A will lead to B are not always correct. These lessons take open minds and hearts. These are not in any particular order. All matter equally to me.

Knowledge is not the same as knowing.

I learned about slavery and Jim Crow. I learned about the Klan and lynching. I learned about Emit Till and Rosa Parks. Surely, I learned about the separate water fountains and lunch counters in the south. Didn't I learn about Martin and Malcolm? I learned some James Baldwin and Langston Hughes, some Toni Morrison and some Nikki Giovanni, some Cornel West and some Tavis Smiley. I thought I learned allot about the experience of being Black in America.

Then I knew La Fonda. My friend taught me the difference between some knowledge and some knowing by letting me get to know her. One day in the office, she told me she hated being told she looked young. Huh? What woman over 35 doesn't like being told she looks young? Apparently, for my friend it means she must have been a black teenage mother in the "accusers" mind. She wanted the world to know she was a college graduate, married and 30 when she had her son. This story isn't shared with white people she meets; only with those that she **KNOWS**!

During another conversation, we discussed her upcoming trip to Tennessee to attend a track meet with her young son. I suggested she go see Dolly Parton's house as I had done when I drove cross-country to move to California. "How were the sightseeing side trips?" I asked when she returned. "Well, Kari Sue, I saw some confederate flags and then noticed there weren't any turnarounds in the center meridians between lanes on the roads. I was not taking a chance with my son in the car that some racist would chase me down and I wouldn't have a turnaround lane for escape", she replied.

Huh? I may check the gas gage and my tire level before a road trip. I am certain that I never considered checking a map to see if the road had a turnaround every few miles!

This story isn't shared with white people she meets; only with those she KNOWS! I imagine she thinks whites will tell her she is over-reacting and paranoid. I bet she's right. I heard that story because she knows if she shares it with me she won't be ridiculed. These are the private stories that all white folks need to hear. They help us KNOW.

Comfortable conversation comes faster poking fun at stereotypes about my people first.

At a recent holiday party, I was having one of those civil and surface conversations with a couple of African American women. I told them my daughter had a sweet 16 at our home the night before with friends from sleep away camp and that a few of the girls and boys slept over. "In the same room?" one asked me with a bit of surprise crossing her face. "Yes, sure! This was a *Jewish camp* sleepover after all. Those boys can be a bit behind, mommy's boys, you know." Laughter; ice is broken. We are allowed to poke fun at our own tribe and only our own tribe. Of course, feel free to poke fun at your own kid, your own age, your own parents, your own knowledge level and your own financial status. Take a chance. Ask one of your black friends why all the skinny white girls sit together in the cafeteria.

It is my responsibility to be more aware of my words and actions as a white person interacting with a person of color than they must be with me.

Life as a white woman has given me privilege that may not be in my conscious awareness. I knock on any door in my neighborhood and expect it to open and the person within to greet me with a smile. I have always been encouraged to ask anyone a question as an equal, that person could be my first grade teacher, a policeman on the street, a doctor or my college professor. I don't have any sense memory that people will be at all suspicious of me. I trot right up to the counter in any store and get within inches of the salesperson's face without any sort of flinching from them. There is no need for me to remember to speak softly or keep my hands at my side. It is not true for many people of color in a majority white city. I know some of those daily activities could be more nerve wracking or dangerous for black folks. I know now that I can represent some of those people who have judged and discredited, who have followed and questioned. It is my job to be more careful and patient. It is, I believe, a small price to pay for my privilege.

However, I assumed this discomfort greatly decreased when the black person in question was a member of the upper class, highly educated, highly respected and integrated into the world of the wealthy and the world of the intellectual elite of all ethnicities. Apparently, not at all times. Recently, I was listening to Clifton Talbot, PhD speak about an experience he had as a dinner guest in a white woman's large upper class home in North Carolina. In his book, "The Invitation", he describes his experience that evening:

"I was a guest at an antebellum mansion in North Carolina. I had to go to the bathroom. I had to go so bad that it was difficult to focus on the conversation. Yet, I was frozen. I couldn't ask to use the white person's toilet. In my mind I was seven years old. I saw the beautiful Chrystal bell on that massive dining table, a dining table set gloriously in my honor! All I could think of was don't ring that bell. I don't want to see my mother come out of that kitchen as a servant."

It is difficult for me to comprehend that a person of such stature could easily regress to feeling like the servant's child, standing in the corner, having to urinate, yet knowing he must hold it silently till his mom could take him outside. I try to get in touch with a childhood memory that affects my rational behavior in the present. The best that comes to mind is the escalator. When I was five my mother told me to hold tight when we got on a department store escalator. She said my cousin Raymond lost his finger playing on an escalator because he wasn't paying attention. From that moment, I have hesitated approaching the moving stairway. There is often a line of people that includes my embarrassed daughter behind me as I do this dance before I finally… STEP ON.

This moment of paralyzing terror comes each and every time. Imagine if it was me that lost the finger? I never so much as tripped while grabbing that rail as if jumping between two tall buildings. Thinking about my irrational fear helps me understand a bit of the experience of Dr. Talbot. It helps me understand why a place, a question or a comment can bring forth discomfort to a person in a way that may not make immediate sense to me. It doesn't have to make sense to me. The popular therapist and spiritualist on the Oprah Winfrey Network, Iyanla Vansant, calls this "cellular memory". She explains that many people of color have suffered these traumas early and often in their lives. The feelings of fear and inferiority can travel through generations. The feeling moves from the memory part of the brain to the emotional part in lightening speed when a threat is perceived. The mind has to work diligently to get that spark of fire back to the rational and thinking brain where we are able to question the veracity of the fear, pain or disgust. Often, it's just too little too late!

My white face can represent "on a cellular" level, the slights, fear, anger or insecurities experienced or witnessed in the past by this individual. I know when the escalator is coming and can prepare. I know I am able to go without seeing one for long periods. Blacks and Latinos in Los Angeles are not able to avoid contact with white people the way I can avoid an escalator. We often represent power, privilege, arrogance and easy living. Sometimes it's true. Sometimes it's a stereotype. I believe it's my responsibility to be cognizant of the possibility that I am seen this way. The remembrance of a hurtful encounter when powerless can sour a person in future encounters with others that remind them of that moment. The reminder may appear simply because of the way someone looks or sounds, but can trigger that hot faced burn of resentment even still.

I heard an interview on the radio with Rick Sanchez after he was fired from CNN a few years back for incidents in which he called talk show host Jon Stewart, and "other northeastern establishment types like him", bigots for their comments about Latinos and then, during an interview, laughed and sarcastically rolled his eyes when the journalist mentioned that Jews had also suffered intolerance in America. During that interview he shared a story about delivering furniture with his dad when he was a young boy in Miami. They were

delivering to an upscale majority Jewish neighborhood in Boca
Raton. When the woman in the big "fancy" house opened the
door, 9-year-old Rick asked for water. The woman said, "The
hose is over there" directing him to the side yard. When I
heard him tell the story, it was clear to me why he cackled
with contempt at the idea of Jews without power. His image
of Jews is of the people that treated he and his father
poorly. When rattled and angry with Jon Stewart for
satirizing his lack of intelligence on "The Daily Show", his
memories of silent humiliation around "people like that"
likely flooded the emotional (amygdala) portion of his brain.
I understand; for me also, "Boca Raton" is synonymous with
dismissive, powerful and "crass" older Jewish people. It is
the first image that comes to my mind immediately upon
hearing those two words. The image was created during my
first association with the town. Thinking a bit longer, I do
remember great people I knew while living there. The first
reaction comes from my emotional brain. I must access my
rational brain to challenge it. I do not associate Jewish
people in general with my association of Boca Raton. I
imagine that is because I have had many positive experiences
in many places and for many years with other Jewish people.
Mr. Sanchez has not. The initial association stuck for him.
I am a white Jewish woman; I am aware of the stereotypes

about Jews and try to challenge them with my behavior. This may be what is called "white guilt" in some circles. I call it awareness of my image and how it affects my encounters.

Do household workers or delivery people laugh at the awkward, patronizing white lady who brings out glasses and ice for them since hearing the "hose" story? Who knows? If it makes a difference, I would rather make myself look a fool than they feel disrespected or invisible. Our family attended the Quincinera for Lizette, the child of my daughter's nanny. This is a significant coming of age ceremony/celebration for a fifteen-year-old girl in most Latino families. Was anyone watching to see how the white family acted? Who knows? All I knew for certain was we were the only white family of the 250 people invited. If other guests were watching or cared at all, I felt I had a responsibility. For me, that meant we would mingle, dance and eat everything on our plates. We would stay till the end of the party and nobody would say "Did you see those timid white people in the corner making faces about our food?" That was the best I could do to dispel what I likely represent in this setting and it felt like something to me!

When my family hosted a Bat Mitzvah party for our daughter, I thought it important to send a printed invitation to the Jimenez family home, seat them at the honored table with the grandparents and include them in the video montage as important people in my daughters life. Did they feel important? Did they have a nice time? Who knows? It was the best I could do and it felt like something to me!

When the Ferguson verdict was announced the first thing I did was text Shawn, my black male co-worker and friend. I said "Nobody is going to shoot me for walking down the street with stolen cigarillos." He replied, "With me, you would." Did it help him feel any better? Who knows? It was the best I could do at the moment and it felt like something to me!

Only authentic exposure provides authentic experience.

"Talia's terrific! She's raw, bold, willing to take risks and happy to take criticism. There's an authenticity to her, a sense of real-ness that is hard to find sometimes amongst teenagers, amongst people come to that. Talia has the quality of being real. Love that."

I am proud of these comments from my daughters' report card. This particular teacher was not the first to comment on her confidence, authenticity or empathic ability by a teacher or coach. I share them because I know the primary reason that she makes this impression is due to a childhood full of experiences being exposed to, and becoming comfortable with, difference. This has been purposeful. Being with La Fonda and the wide variety of folks with whom I conduct diversity training, brought great richness to my life. La Fonda was in the room when Talia was born. Seeing people from an early age that looked different from her parents happened naturally because of my friend group. I knew she wouldn't scream at the sight of a black lady at her second birthday party the way that little girl screamed at the sight of blue-eyed me a couple of years earlier! Seeing isn't enough. Exposure that results in a sense of comfort and normalcy, is the key component.

Fortunately, I live in a neighborhood that is quite mixed compared to typical suburban communities. It was built in the 1920s, so has residents of various generations. It is in close proximity to LA's largest concentration of gay residents, West Hollywood. This gives our area "spillover" from people that don't want to be in the center of the nightlife prominent in West Hollywood but want to be nearby. It's walk able and central, which attracts young groups of singles renting together. Being walk able and central attracts families interested in a more urban feel. People who like "walk able-urban" tend to come from a mix of ethnicities. The early years required only leaving the house on foot and actually talking to people on the street, in the grocer and at the dry cleaner. Not a tough task for me.

I hired a nanny when I was at work. Many families in Los
Angeles hire home child care employees from Central America.
This is certainly exposure. However, the quality and long -
term effect of this exposure is dependent, in my opinion, on
the message my interaction with this woman gives my child.
Confession... I am a "free range parent" and value
independence and confidence in children highly. Lot's of
parents, black and white, have expressed some level of shock
at my philosophy. I stand by it. To begin with, Norma
doesn't speak English and that was a choice. "What if she
has to call you?" they ask. "You never call her either," they
continue wide eyed. "Nope" is my answer. "She can say baby
sick and hospital. I got a pediatrician that speaks Spanish.
What else is important?" What I mean by this is that when I
walk out the door I hoped she would feel respected and
trusted. She can dress her as she pleases, give her any
lunch that feels right, go to the park on her own or have
other nannies and children over to my house without alerting
me. I believe allowing for these daily choices greatly
contribute to the atmosphere of comfort and respect in our
home and to the loving bond between this woman and my child.

Maybe you, the reader, considers me irresponsible. You
would not be the first! But before judging, ask yourself if
your kid's nanny would risk herself by running in the street

after your child. I know Norma would. She is respected and trusted as the mom in charge when I am not home and acts accordingly. Treat the person responsible for your child as a replaceable employee watched closely for lack of trust and she will also act accordingly! This demonstration of acceptance and respect is not only supposed to relay a message to Talia's caretaker; it is supposed to relay a message to Talia. Qualities valued by my family are the qualities I should value.

As our children grow our "exposure" choices register with them more frequently. They observe with whom we engage. They observe the places we take them to play and go to school. They see with whom we seem uninterested or annoyed? I took this job of wide and varied exposure choices seriously. My husband would say a bit too seriously. Thankfully, my three year old didn't know it was weird to go to Jewish pre-school in the morning, get picked up and then dropped off at a secular pre-school in West Hollywood Park on afternoons. "What synagogue do you go to for Hebrew School?" Jewish parents would ask. "We go to Kol Ami, in West Hollywood," my straight husband and I would answer. "Oh, how nice! Isn't that a gay synagogue?" would be the next perplexed question. "Well, yes, it is majority gay but everyone is welcome."

When it was time for kindergarten, we chose the local public elementary school. I assure you, we are not martyrs! The school rates in the top 10% academically in Los Angeles. However, many of our neighbors were surprised about our choice. "I heard that school is mostly Korean," they would say. "I heard that the Korean parents aren't very friendly and your daughter will be left out of the birthday parties." Of course, none of these folks pitying my poor Caucasian daughter had been to the school. In fact, it was obvious none bothered to check with the publicly available district demographics page on their computer. If they had, they would have known the school is 42% Asian, 28% white, 15%, Black, 10% Latino and 5% other. The "others" are largely international students from India or Africa who are attending while parents are working temporarily in the city in the film business or in medicine at Cedars Sinai hospital around the corner. Hancock Park Elementary is the most ethnically diverse school in L.A. and I can walk there! Walking to school in Los Angeles is far from being a certainty. If you can, it likely has a student demographic comprised of more than 85% White, Black, Latino or Asian. Mixed student populations are rare in most L.A. public schools. This is an obvious result of the rarity of ethnically mixed residential areas in our city. It just happens that this particular school district includes a large apartment complex, Park LaBrea, spread over many acres, offering a wide range of housing choices including furnished units for visiting professionals, 1, 2 or 3 bedroom units in either garden style "villas" or new york style high rises appealing to both families and singles seeking roommates. The development even includes areas designated pet friendly. "Mixed-use development" is a term that is currently in vogue as city planners try to find ways to lessen the environmental impact of suburban sprawl, while hoping to increase contact between neighbors too busy driving to meet each other.

Ironically, this sixty-year-old housing complex built for returning World War Two veterans and their families, is the quintessential example of what mixed use is supposed to be! Amenities include green space with enormous trees, a playground with bar-b-queue, a day care, and a community center, walking distance to both shopping and an elementary school. Park LaBrea has the added benefit, in my opinion, of being home to long time elderly residents in rent controlled apartments and to young singles attracted to the high-rise towers and plentiful amenities. I know these tidbits, because shocking as it seems, Talia has been a guest at countless birthday parties in Park LaBrea hosted by classmates from various cultural backgrounds. She never did mention feeling left out by the "Korean kids." Although, she often took the opportunity to let me know their moms prepared much better lunches for them than I did for her! It seems stereotypical 1st generation Korean culture is heavy on homemade, healthy, and beautifully presented food.

During these elementary school years, while many of our neighbors transported their children by car for hours por day to insure that they attended a comfortable and familiar school where parents spoke unaccented English, Talia was on the playground...PLAYING. This choice worked for our family. We were fortunate to have the choice of attending a public school so close to our home. Most don't have such a choice.

There are other sorts of exposure that are relatively simple in a diverse city. Most parents either aren't aware, or aren't interested, in trying activities they have not heard about from a friend or neighbor that "looks like them". Thus, the segregation continues on all sides. There was a seemingly non-stop conversation occupying a majority of parents in the schoolyard, the market and in the park. "Where do you live?" is how it begins. Within 15 minutes, you knew about all the "best" pediatricians, pre-schools, parks, soccer leagues, art classes, theater camps and birthday party performers you could ever contact. I have no beef with these people until someone laments "My child doesn't have any diversity in their friend group. I wish L.A. wasn't so divided by ethnic areas. In New York you see all kinds of folks every day. You can't even walk in this city."

It is true that driving is often a necessity in our city. It is also true that a drive to an isolated canyon park in Beverly Hills takes more time than a drive to a public park in Santa Monica or Venice. It is true that all your kids' friends are going to ballet in one studio. It is also true that the parks and rec calendar has ballet classes happening all over the city. One does not have to be a renegade to be sure to plan a bit of both.

For instance, our summer calendar included a 3-week camp at an exclusive private school. This cost $350 per week. That was followed by 3 weeks at the local park camp. This costs $80.00 per week. Next, 2 weeks at the "Youth Academy of Dramatic Arts" for performance. That one cost a whopping $450 per week. Finally, there was a 2-week dance intensive at Lula Washington Dance Theater at a cost of $125 per week. The costlier camps had participants that were generally wealthy, and majority white. The public park camp was mixed socio-economically and culturally. Lula Washington Dance theater was majority black and in a working class area off Crenshaw Blvd. This was a normal and expected summer for Talia for five years running.

After a few years she noticed that friends at the lower
cost camps stayed at the same place all summer long. She also
noticed the friends at the higher cost camps spent two weeks
in Europe with family every year, ate at fancy restaurants,
and went to Disneyland on a whim. We talked about these
visible differences. She got the rare experience of feeling
both jealous *and* fortunate. I believe both are necessary for
full development. Both are necessary exposures in order to
normalize ones experiences as sometimes "not as good as" and
sometimes "better than." No, Talia's Nanny's daughter didn't
have her own room, but she could find friends in the hallway
anytime and invited my kid to lots of parties filled with
dancing, delicious food and fun cousins. They were described
as "way more fun" than our parties. Our daughter didn't have
a pool or a "microphone gate" at her house like her friend
Danielle, but could ride her bike down the street in our
neighborhood; Danielle couldn't because in her neighborhood
the houses were too far apart and there weren't any
sidewalks. We are absolutely convinced these parenting
choices helped our child develop into the *"raw, bold and
authentic girl"* her instructor says she is.

It's not always about race

The cultural competency training programs we conduct begin
with one of a variety of exercises designed to get
participants to reflect deeply on their entire identity. One
of these, the multicultural tree worksheet, focuses on our
history, influences and hopes for the future. The tree is a
helpful metaphor with roots representing our past, the trunk
our strength, the branches being the connections and groups
to which we belong and buds our future dreams. Another is
called identity stew. Participants must choose the four most
important factors of many possibilities listed that have
contributed to creating their personal identity or "stew."
These four are literally cut from the list and placed in a
bowl. It requires reflection and prioritizing. Certainly for
most people, the strongest identification is with the racial,
ethnic and religious aspects of their lives. However, during
the course of filling out these sheets alone and then
verbally sharing answers and reasons for one's answers with
the five others in their assigned round table grouping,
something unexpected occurs. Individuals discover that

culture is often more than what we see. It is more than skin color, gender or age. Long held beliefs and values associated with our profession, personal interests and skills, socio-economic status, geography and family size can contribute greatly create to our cultural identity.

We have witnessed tablemates who look, speak and dress so differently from each other that it seems unlikely they would find common ground, suddenly become culturally connected through the discovery that they each have six siblings. The two share an experience few have shared and are able to form a bond happily discussing those seemingly universal commonalities of life in a big family that sound as foreign to the rest of us listening to this shorthand banter, as it might be hearing them speak to one another in a language from "the old country", a language long dormant, then suddenly brought joyously back to life! We believe that by encouraging this sort of exploration and expansion of the typical definition of culture, we can bring an additional opportunity for connection. A Cultural connection need not result in friendship or even in positive feelings toward another. Rather, the primary goal in finding cultural connection is to bring humanity to the other during the encounter.

We find that utilizing our cultural identity questionnaire is a surprisingly helpful tool for relieving the discomfort many feel when opening up to unfamiliar others. It is as if they are telling themselves: "The questions are created by the facilitator; we all have the same questions and our assignment requires that we answer them as fully as possible. We can't be accused of inappropriate prying, after all."

Students often tell us after completing this initial segment, that our use of pre-printed questions, coupled with specific directions for the order and style of sharing, helped to reduce feelings of anxiety about what to say. We instruct students to sit at circular tables of five. First, everyone writes down the answers silently with an understanding that nobody else will read their paper. Following this self-reflective writing, we ask for one volunteer at each table to be the first to verbally share whatever they like from their answer to the first cultural history question with the other four. The first one volunteering tends to be the least shy or nervous, thus setting the tone for all. Each person at the table reveals their response to the first question before moving on to the second question and so on… until all are finished. The rules are designed to prevent the "big talkers" from taking over the room and to keep the "small talkers" from disappearing.

Requiring this amount of specificity may seem excessive; it isn't! Adults are far more self-conscious than children when contemplating the way others perceive them. Possibly, they have been rebuffed or embarrassed in the past. "I don't want to say the wrong thing. It's not worth the risk" is the mantra-like phrase ringing in the subconscious. These fears cause many of us to stay away from conversations that venture below the surface. The possibility of discomfort keeps most folks firmly within established boundaries of safe, familiar and culturally comfortable environments rather than venturing toward the unknown. This behavior results in a loss of the possibility of discovering a less "obvious" area of cultural connection with another person simply because we don't "look" like we fit together.

Expanding and exploring the concept of belonging to multiple cultures is not only about connection; it is also about our aversions. Our identities are comprised of so many pieces. Many of the pieces are subject to stereotype. Many of these stereotypes disrupt our sense of self in conscious and subconscious ways. This phenomenon is what Claude Steele describes vividly in his book "Whistling Vivaldi":

"We could all take out a piece of paper, write down the major stereotypes of many identities in society and show a high degree of agreement in what we wrote. This means that whenever we are in a situation where a bad stereotype about one of our own identities could be applied to us — such as those about being old, poor, rich, or female- we know it. We know what people could think. We know that anything we do that fits this stereotype could be taken as confirming it. And we know that, for that reason, we could be judged and treated accordingly. That's why it's a standard human

predicament. In one form or another—be it through the threat of a stereotype about having lost memory capacity or being cold in relations with others—it happens to us all, perhaps several times a day. It is present in any situation to which a stereotype is relevant. And this means that it follows members of the stereotyped group in these situations like a balloon over their heads." He calls it stereotype threat or identity threat and says it is hard to shake.

Could this explain why Kari is petrified every time she approaches a movie ticket seller since being asked a year ago if she was a senior? Is she an old lady? Might it be the reason she will not even glance down at a restaurant receipt after dinner for fear that someone will think she is a cheap Jew? Maybe identity threat is the prominent feeling La Fonda experiences when other Black women inquire about her marital status at her son's private school. They think I am another single Black woman after their man. She doesn't feel that familiar hot-faced discomfort when asked the same question by a white woman. Do we feel stereotype threat even when we have displayed in every rational way that the stereotype doesn't fit our behavior? Sometimes we do! Kari tells a story she finds humorous and revealing.

"A couple of years back, I conducted cultural competency training with another consultant from our office, Shawn. We headed to a residential drug rehabilitation center in Pomona to deliver a half-day seminar and drove together. The manager was kind enough to serve lunch and invite Shawn and I to join. The dining table was full with platters of bologna, ham and American cheese. There was bright yellow mustard, white bread and red Kool-Aid. I looked over at Shawn and he looked over at me. No words spoken between us, but without a doubt, this black gay man and this white straight woman were

62

thinking the same thought. "If we touch that bologna sandwich
we will immediately be transported to our respective kitchens
of origin." These kitchens have flowered wallpaper, olive
green refrigerators, cracked linoleum floors fashioned into a
brick pattern and sticky squeaky vinyl covered chairs around
the peeling wood veneer table. We couldn't go back there! We
politely told the manager "Thank you, but we need to get back
to the office." We jumped in the car and headed to Carl's
Junior. The two of us were happy to eat from a taco truck.
We weren't snobs. This wasn't about fancy. This was about
the food we grew up with. We were cool west coast city folk
now! Our status so fragile that eating bologna, white bread
and French's mustard would bring us back to that soulless
suburb in our heads."

This obsession with wanting to be interesting and

different is irrational! Eating food fraught with childhood

associations won't make us "regular". Yet, this crazy fear

has bonded us, given us a private language and lots of

laughter. In fact, we called each other laughing hysterically

after watching a recent episode of the ABC show "Blackish."

In the episode, the dad, Andre, takes his family out to

dinner at a favorite childhood eatery. This place held fond

memories of special family outings for Andre. He wanted to

share the experience with his wife and kids. The place was

called "Beef Plantation." It was strikingly similar to a

Sizzler or Hometown Buffet. From the moment the fictional

Johnson family entered, the judgmental remarks flew. His

young daughter wondered why the food was covered with a

plastic roof and said the meat was "sad looking." His ten

years old son couldn't eat a bite, even though he claimed he was starving. This man felt rejected by his own family; his own Black family. It wasn't a racial experience dividing them. It was socio-economic status and lifestyle. The Johnson family associated The Beef Plantation with low quality. They assumed dad was just too stingy to take them out for a nice meal. Andre associated it with abundant food and family fun. Shawn and I understood where these kids were coming from. Poor Andre was experiencing unintended identity threat and was despondent. The rejection of the meal was not really a rejection of him, but felt that way non-the less.

In a 2008 article for the *American Scholar Magazine*, William Deresiewicz, writes about an epiphany he had standing in his kitchen with a white male there to fix the pipes.

" It didn't dawn on me that there might be a few holes in my education until I was about 35. I'd just bought a house, the pipes needed fixing, and the plumber was standing in my kitchen. There he was, a short, beefy guy with a goatee and a Red Sox cap and a thick Boston accent, and I suddenly learned that I didn't have the slightest idea what to say to someone like him. So alien was his experience to me, so unguessable his values, so mysterious his very language that I couldn't succeed in engaging him in a few minutes of small talk before he got down to work. Fourteen years of higher education and a handful of Ivy League degrees and there I was, stiff and stupid, struck by my own dumbness. "Ivy retardation," a friend of mine calls this. I could carry on conversations with people from other countries in other languages, but I couldn't talk to a man who was standing in my own house."

The quote is from an article handed out to the parent participants at a lecture on "Interpreting the PSAT" at a Los Angeles private school. I think the well-intentioned parent supplying the article hoped to get the others to recognize the downside of Elite universities; trying to soften the blow that most of their offspring will not be attending one. Best to begin with the mindset "Who needs an Ivy anyway"

We saw the self-deprecating admission from the author differently. Our initial thoughts were "Why is this guy realizing this *now*? Has he really never had a workman in his presence? Not a housekeeper or gardener? Are there no food service workers, janitors or landscapers at Yale?" We were stunned that this realization came to him at 35 and so many thought it a profound insight! Then we decided it best to put our self-righteous judgment aside and acknowledge his was a brave admission. We came to agree that late is, in fact, better than never…MUCH BETTER! We also thought about the gentleman in the Red Sox cap with the Boston accent, he likely noticed the discomfort of the Ivy professor. He may have felt the sting of one of those micro-aggressions described earlier by Claudia Rankine, or felt nothing at all. In fact, this stereotype plumber with Red Sox cap and Boston accent may have had no interest in chatting up the stereotype sockless topsiders and chinos Yale guy anyway!

The professor chastises himself for his myopic self described "Ivy Retardation" during the encounter. His article describes vast advantages available to members of that insulated world. Many arrive having taken for granted the benefits of what these two authors call "Ivy admiration."

It's a bit like white privilege: a general sense of safety

and well being in most settings. It is a feeling experienced

for the first time by supreme court justice Sonia Sotomayor

upon her acceptance to Princeton University in the 70s. She

shares a vivid and enlightening account in her book "My

Beloved World" when out with her mother shopping for a coat

that she would take with her to college.

" I'd never cared enough to fall in love with a garment. But
wrapped in this, I knew I wouldn't feel so odd away at
school. Unfortunately, it was a size too small. I tried on a
couple of other coats, but my heart had been claimed, and
Mami knew it. I was ready to leave and try elsewhere, but she
said, "Espera... Sonia, wait, maybe they can order it."
She went to the counter and waited in silence as the
saleswoman helped another customer. And then another and
another. My mother is a very patient woman, so I knew what
it finally took for her to say, "Miss, I need help."
"What do you want?" she snapped without turning.
"Do you have this in a twelve?"
"If it's not on the rack, we don't have it."
"Do you have another store? Can you order it?"
The woman finally turned and looked at her. "Well that would
be a lot of trouble, wouldn't it?" I was halfway out the
door, fully expecting my mother to give up, but she stood her
ground. "I know it's a lot of trouble, but my daughters
going away to college and she likes this coat. Would you
please go and look to see if you can find this coat?" Her
silent shrug spoke loudly: You're a pain in the ass. She
turned away indifferently, and asked:
"So where's she going to college?"
"To Princeton", Mommie said. Sotomayor writes: "I saw the
woman's head swing around as in a cartoon double take. The
transformation was remarkable. She was suddenly all courtesy
and respect, full of praise for Princeton, and more than
happy to make a call in search of my coat, which, as it turns
out, arrived in a week. I commented to my mother on the
woman's change of attitude. My mother stopped in the shadow
of the elevated track and said to me, I have to tell you
Sonia, at the hospital I'm being treated like a queen right

now. Doctors who never once had a nice word for me, who have never spoken to me at all, have come up to congratulate me."

When a person has not experienced invisibility or disregard based on the way they look or speak, it is difficult to recognize what feels different about privilege. Justice Sotomajor has participated fully in life on both sides of the tracks. She has used this rare and valuable gift of "knowing" along with vast knowledge to inform her decisions and interactions for the better of us all!

Most people are conditioned to seek the approval of the more "powerful" individual in any exchange. It is worth considering why we felt badly for the plumber in the Dereseiwicz article and not for the author. Certainly, most of us did. The more "powerful" often means the one with the ability to get us a job or an introduction. The less powerful can be invisible and meaningless. On rare occasion, the invisible party does indeed get noticed and finds themself able to have a bit of justice with the Goliath in their presence. Being Democrats, we admit to being delighted when a bartender, Scott Prouty, secretly recorded Mitt Romney's infamous 47% comments during a $50,000 per plate campaign fundraiser in Boca Raton, Fla. in May 2012. Romney said:

"There are 47 percent of the people who will vote for the president no matter what. All right, there are 47 percent who are with him, who are dependent upon government, who believe that they are victims, who believe the government has a responsibility to care for them, who believe that they are

entitled to health care, to food, to housing, to you-name-it.
That's an entitlement. The government should give it to them.
And they will vote for this president no matter what. And I
mean the president starts off with 48, 49...he starts off
with a huge number. These are people who pay no income tax.
Forty-seven percent of Americans pay no income tax. So our
message of low taxes doesn't connect. So he'll be out there
talking about tax cuts for the rich. ... My job is not to
worry about those people. I'll never convince them they
should take personal responsibility and care for their lives.
What I have to do is convince the 5—10% in the center that
are independents, that are thoughtful, that look at voting
one way or the other depending upon in some cases emotion,
whether they like the guy or not."

The comments are familiar to many of us. However, the reason

for the release of the recording is not so well known. Few of

us of have heard Mr. Prouty describe why he allowed Mother

Jones magazine to print what he heard. We haven't heard him

describe the difference in experience he had when serving

President Bill Clinton a soda and Mitt Romney a soda at a

fundraising event. In the Clinton encounter, he was thanked

for the drink. When the evening concluded, Mr. Clinton went

into the kitchen to stop for photos with the wait staff.

This was a five-minute detour. He was noticed. In the Romney

encounter, the bartender was not thanked nor acknowledged in

any way. He was invisible. He was angry.

It is mistaken to believe that the Yale professor, a

plumber or the presidential candidate is required to have

lunch or a philosophical discussion with someone that lives a

very different every day life. There are times those

discussions work, but mostly they are a bit awkward. We are allowed to choose our friends from those with whom we share common interests. Preferences do not make us elitist snobs. Disregard makes us snobs. Disregard is sometimes displayed by people who are unaware they are showing it at all!

Recently, we sat in on a "Council" with students and teachers at a local school. This is a class in which all sit in a circle as equals while taking turns speaking and listening "from the heart". The person speaking holds a "talking piece", assuring no interruption until they finish and pass it on to the next member of the circle. The process is designed to create a trusting environment in which all are equally important. During this particular council, we listened to a teacher tell the group about her pride in choosing a career in teaching rather than Law, the career her family pressured her to pursue. When she spoke the word "lawyer" she put her finger down her throat in that universally recognized "gagging" reflex we make when thoroughly disgusted by something. We wondered if anyone in the room had a parent or friend that practiced law? Think they felt disregarded? We do.

Kari's daughter, Talia, came home from school in third grade and announced in shock "Mom, I met a McCain and she was actually nice!" Was Kari speaking with disregard during that presidential campaign about Republicans? Most definitely! Disregard is never necessary!

All of us must examine these feelings of rejection and insecurity when they happen. We must examine the times we seem to reject certain others and the times certain others seem to reject us. It truly does help to think a moment when these *"flashes"* of contempt occur. Ask yourself "Why did that comment or look trigger my internal alarm? Was a slight intended? Have I made that sort of mistake with others? Should I address it, ignore it with residual anger, or ignore it and move on with life?"

Some of our internalized stereotypes are humorous; others are the source of discomfort felt, or anger directed, toward another. All are normal feelings of bias that need not create defensiveness, denial or shame for the individual experiencing the emotion. Instead, these "flashes" ought to bring reflection, acknowledgement and change when possible.

Taking it to the streets

White people had to listen in 2014. We had to listen as
young unarmed Black men were shot and killed in quick
succession by White police officers and "wanna be" police
officers, as was the case with George Zimmerman. We had to
listen because the media finally made us listen. In the cases
of Tamir Rice and Eric Garner we had to listen *AND* watch.
Many of us were surprised at the lack of punishment the
shooters received. Others tried to explain away the police
actions as warranted fear and self defense.

Thankfully, the large, peaceful and racially mixed marches
in our cities allowed the world to see that not all white
people agreed with the decisions of the grand jury in
Ferguson and New York. We paid more attention. We listened as
the talking head attorneys on TV schooled the naïve about the
intricacies of grand jury decisions. We learned that the
prosecutor controls the hearing, has a co-dependent
relationship with the police and does not allow defense
attorneys to question witnesses. It was schooling that was
long overdue for the dominant and wealthier groups in

society. It seems a fair assumption that more whites in 2015 will know about the dangers inherent in being a Black male than in 2014. More will likely know that DWB stands for driving while Black. More will know that the "stop and frisk" policy in New York has disproportionately targeted black males. More will have heard that drug related arrests and incarcerations of Blacks are far greater than those given to Whites for the same offense. Finally, as the naïve among us begin to believe and digest the facts of our policing and criminal justice systems, we will use the knowledge to create change in these uneven and racist policies. Crisis can create change. Often it's the *ONLY* thing that creates change.

It took the firebombing deaths of four little girls in a church in Alabama to break the inertia during the early civil rights movement. It took televised beatings on the William Pettis Bridge in Selma to move congress forward on voting rights. It took the senseless police killings in the summer of 2014 of Mike Brown, Eric Garner and Tamir Rice, to get us to believe there is any problem with the law enforcement policy directed at people of color in this country, and it took the massacre at a black church in South Carolina carried out by a white supremist to galvanize state government to take the confederate flag from state House grounds.

We are encouraged by current discussions in the halls of power and at the dinner tables of previously unaffected and unaware citizens. We are hopeful that more research and resources will be provided to address this urgent problem. We look forward to witnessing change that is noticeable and real. We hope to contribute to this change by sharing stories of engagement in our worlds, separately and together.

Charles Blow, a columnist with the New York Times and celebrated author, published an OP-ED in December of 2014 titled "The Obamas, Race and Slights." He relays a couple of stories Mrs. Obama shared in an interview with a journalist from People Magazine:

She told of being asked to get something off the shelf by a customer in a Target store. She said being seen as someone who could give assistance is nothing new and part of life. Blow wonders aloud the way many white people do: "Could the Target shopper who asked Mrs. Obama for help simply not have recognized her and needed, presumably, a taller persons assistance?" Maybe. Or, as Blow offers, could the encounter have been disdainful and presumptuous, a manifestation of some inherent bias? Sure. "The truth is", he reminds the reader, "We don't know." The lady asking for help might not even know. We are not always aware of our biases, let alone are we always able to articulate them. For Mrs. Obama, it is a feeling." Charles Blow then explains vividly what the feeling is. "These are feelings that are informed by facts, experiences, conditioning and culture, but the feelings are what linger, questions of malice and motive hanging in the air like the stench of rotting meat, knotting the stomach and chilling the skin."

Those of us who haven't felt *"the feeling"* have a tough time understanding it. Kari will likely always feel relief when a cop pulling her over calls her by her first name. This fact registered in her mind: "He likes me, No ticket." A person of color will likely feel disrespected when a police officer addresses them by their first name during the exact same type of encounter. Alvin Puissant, a professor of psychiatry at Harvard Medical School, describes using this informal speech as akin to calling a black man "Boy" He explains the titles Mr. and Mrs. or Sir and Madame were never used to address black people. Therefore, using ones first name too soon is seen as too intimate and possibly disrespectful for many people of color. Some of these experiences just register differently internally.

The "Taking it to the streets" portion of our project is focused on describing our reaction to these encounters with others. Do these internal sensations register differently for us separately, than they do when we are together? What happens emotionally for us in familiar settings compared with those felt in unfamiliar settings? Are we able to describe what happens with clarity? Readers may recall the highly publicized incident of racial humiliation described by Oprah Winfrey, the beloved talk-show host and philanthropist, while she shopped in an upscale boutique in Europe. When Winfrey asked to see a bag with a $38,000 price tag, the store clerk told her the purse was too expensive for her while redirecting her gaze to a less expensive item. She told the story so that we might be educated that not everyone is greeted the same in "high priced" establishments. Winfrey graciously, and without anger, explains the comment:

"I was referencing it as an example of being in a place where people don't expect that you would be able to be there. I purposely did not mention the name of the store. I'm sorry that I said it was Switzerland."

We imagine Ms. Winfrey did not come across as angry, because she was not surprised. She didn't want the woman, or her country, to be ridiculed. Instead, she wanted us to understand that the saleswoman's attitude was not uncommon. Winfrey additionally took pains to explain that she was not wearing clothing or jewelry that may have given the clerk a "tip off" as to her ability to buy a purse that costs thousands. In this way, she allows her audience a kind of racism "out". Certainly, in our hearts, we knew her skin color was a factor, but she didn't have to say it out loud. She got us to *consider the possibility*. It is this uniquely gentle, yet honest, approach that elicits the trust and affection Oprah Winfrey deservedly receives!

Maybe, you have heard a friend or acquaintance of color describe what it's like for them to be followed by employees in a similar establishment. Maybe you expressed shock, anger or sadness on hearing the story, but will you ever knowingly and consciously feel the difference of not being followed, of not being viewed with suspicion? Is it even possible?

We decided to add another criteria to our experiment. In addition to observing and recording the interactions experienced "in the streets" by La Fonda alone, and by us together, Kari would try to be more cognizant of her daily interactions as a white woman; in other words, be vigilantly attentive to the life she has known and never questioned. This could prove to be a clever way to heighten the awareness of a sometimes-skeptical white community to the reality of "white privilege" afforded them nearly every day. CONSCIOUS WHITENESS is the term used by the anti-racist educator, and author, Tim Wise, to label this pursuit. It's radical; we know! Kari will have to stop, think, reflect, and record, the stuff she has done and said unconsciously, and automatically, her entire life. She will never truly know if her encounters or assumptions would be different if she were of another ethnicity. In fact, she will not know if what she feels would be any different if she were younger, older, fatter, gay or male. You will have to judge and compare these stories with your recollection of being involved in similar situations while living in your skin and the package that surrounds it.

It wasn't long before the "ah ha" moments of white lady consciousness started to take hold. She hired an upholsterer to redo a chair. She wrote a check to Hector Ramirez, closed the door and sat in her new chair. Minutes later Mr. Ramirez called from the local bank. "They wouldn't cash my check. Can you come and meet me with cash?" he wanted to know. She tells Fonda the story:

"I was driving over and seething over the fact that an honest Latino man couldn't get his check cashed at Wells Fargo. I assumed he didn't have a checking account or I.D. I thought about how he would have to pay enormous interest at a check-cashing place. So unfair, I thought! It didn't occur to me that he probably wouldn't have taken a check in the first place if he were forced to use a check cashing store rather than a bank! It didn't enter my mind that it could be *ME* that bounced a check. I was wrong! It turns out I did bounce the check. Someone had stolen a previously mailed check, changed the amount and cleaned out my account. The account had been empty for a couple of days. Interesting though, the bank did cash another check while it was empty. The other check was made out to a tutor, Lenore Barker. She, too, came inside the bank to cash her check. She is a white woman, tall, slender and elegant looking, and with a British accent. Hmmm… I think I am starting to see the world differently practicing this conscious whiteness thing. First, I thought about my quick assumption that the Latino guy had no checking account. Second, I mentally filed the fact that a check written to Hector Ramirez was not cashed but Linda's was. Finally, I was aware this banker never doubted my insistence that I couldn't have bounced a check, and how quickly he refunded my money while another employee got busy bringing me coffee and cookies; just normal life in a bank as Kari Bower, the white, married and middle aged woman!"

On another occasion, she goes to Ross Dress for Less, a favorite discount chain for home goods and clothing. She considers herself on assignment, spending time "Shopping While White", with acutely open eyes and ears. She hangs out by the pillows in the back of the store where the security guard is supposed to ask to see the receipts of those exiting with bags. He does ask four of the five Black women that leave to show their receipt. He does not stop the Black woman with two children. He stops two white teenage girls, but none of the other three white women. He stops one middle aged Latino looking man with a young boy. He does not stop two mid-aged Asian women shopping together. Kari reports:

"I bought a big pillow so as not to get a bag from the cashier. I walk out the door with the receipt in my purse, not visible, clutching the giant pillow to my belly. I didn't look at the guy and he didn't stop me."

She assures me this is an everyday occurrence for her in the world of "Shopping While White!" She chose this location because of the robust mix of people from various ethnic groups she often sees in the store. This is not one of those expensive boutiques in Beverly Hills where a sales clerk may be so accustomed to the "stereotypical" white bejeweled female customer, that one with a different physical profile sets off an automatic trigger of discomfort for the employee. Why the bias in this place? How deeply ingrained are these assumptions? Do they enter our mind even when attempting to practice conscious whiteness? Kari recalled a recent comment proving her biased assumptions are sometimes on the tip of her tongue:

"Can you believe I come out of a movie and give the valet my ticket only to find out some lady backed into my door while it was parked at the valet stand! He got her information. At least we know a lady with the name Janet Goldstein has auto insurance, right?"

We both giggled with recognition. Obviously, both of us registered the same automatic bias at the same time. Jewish drivers have money and thus, car insurance!

For one of our group outings, we decided to attend the opening of a new restaurant with another black girl friend, Tracee. It was a reasonably priced place aimed at serving the lunch crowd a quick, but not "fast food" style meal. The quick part was ordering at a counter; the restaurant part was the variety of freshly made items brought to us at our chic rustic table, under the Edison style string of bulbs, illuminating glossy red walls covered in vintage black and white photos. Quintessential L.A. cool!

We started eating our little deep fried pockets filled with all kinds of ingredients, really tasty and lots of fun. Kari had an extra item on her plate and asked the other girls: "Where is your complementary desert? Didn't the person at the counter offer you a Ball of Love? It's deep fried ice cream with chocolate sauce". "Ah, no, of course not", was the simultaneous answer from La Fonda and Tracee. "The girl at the counter is black; black servers always treat the whites better!" They did both say it at the same moment... Maybe there is some truth to the theory after all. Valuable research and a Ball of Love; can't beat that!

We decided to walk around and get desert for the two *"neglected ones"* in our party elsewhere. Unfortunately, our elsewhere was a popular bakery with a long line of people outside the door. We waited and waited. The "neglected" two spied a table full of snacks nearby intended for the film crew in the *building. It started as a joke; "Kari, go snatch us something off that table. You're a white girl. Nobody will try to stop you."*
She wouldn't do it, arguing the food was there for anybody, and if they were so hungry, they could grab a bag of cookies too, the white thing was ridiculous. Tracee and La Fonda got serious. "No really; we can't take anything, but you can. Please, just an Oreo or something, we're starving!" The big white savior walked up to the table, got some Oreos, and said hello to the folks from the film crew sitting around. Nobody blinked; her black friends swore that would not have happened for them. These internalized feelings about what may occur in a given situation are powerful reminders of the long history of oppression. This Maya Angelou quote beautifully explains how quickly those feelings surface in the soul:

 "I've learned that people will forget what you said, people will forget what you did, but people will never forget how you made them feel."

Opening The Doors

1903- W.E.B. Dubois

"In a world where it means so much to take a man by the hand and sit beside him, to look frankly into his eyes and feel his heart beating with red blood, in a world where a social cigar or a cup of tea together means more than legislative halls-one can imagine the consequences of the almost utter absence of social amenities between such estranged races whose separation extends even to parks and streetcars"

1963- Martin Luther King

"After a century of Jim Crow, we hated and feared each other because we didn't know each other. Knowing each other, sustained intergroup, interpersonal doing, was the only way to undo the damage of not knowing each other."

1994- Rodney King-

"People Can we all get along?"

1997- President William Jefferson Clinton

On proposing a national dialogue on race..."Take personal responsibility for reaching out to people of different races, take time to sit down and talk through the issue, have the courage to speak honestly and frankly, and then have the discipline to listen quietly with an open mind as others do the same."

2009- Attorney General Eric Holder

"When it comes to racism, America is a nation of cowards. Certain subjects are off-limits and that to explore them risks at best embarrassment, and at worst, the questioning of one's character."

2014- Writer, Producer and Activist Norman Lear

"What we don't do is talk about race. What we don't do is open our eyes and our hearts to a conversation about it."

The previous celebrated quotes represent over 100 years of acknowledgement on the part of well-known American icons that *KNOWING* is not a side benefit of improved race relations; it is *CENTRAL* to them! The two of us have explained the difference between knowing and knowledge in our own encounters and friendships. Is *"KNOWING"* an unfamiliar person such a monumental task? It seems so for most of us. Is it worth the discomfort and fumbling when we are unsure in our approach and conversation? We believe the effort worth it if it honestly matters to you.

For some, it matters professionally. This is often the case for those who are minorities both in population number and in access to professional opportunity. For others, it matters personally. These individuals desire a more diverse circle of people in their lives. Statistics are clear; our eyes don't deceive us; we actually see very few ethnically mixed tables in the cafeterias and social events of our lives. Comfort, acceptance, and trust, are paramount for folks who live much of their day navigating a world that often brings forth feelings of discomfort and distrust; why not seek familiarity now and then?

When we see a gathering of people "over there", an internal alarm sends the message: "They looks like me, dress like me and eat like me; I am attracted to that group." It isn't crazy, nor is it shameful, to feel this way! On the other hand, in private conversation, so many profess sincere interest in walking over to the other part of the room, to the group that seems unfamiliar in looks and style. We think about taking a chance. We want to open the doors. We want to learn. We want to laugh. We want to talk. We want to do these things, but want to do them well. We need help!

While researching this book, we read other peoples stories of friendship across the color line. Something jumped out at us. The cross cultural interactions that developed into that elusive *KNOWING, seemed to* start early in life and occurred frequently. Bill Clinton, affectionately called "The First Black President" by the renown writer Toni Morrison in her description of his background and cultural style, explains his interpretation of the odd title to Charles Barkley during an interview for Barkley's book: "Who is Afraid of a Large Black Man":

"Growing up in Arkansas shaped my political views in several ways. First, when I was a little boy hanging out in my grandfathers store, I became aware of his commitment to treating everyone the same whether they had money or not. Even though it was during segregation, my grandparents store served customers of all races. I spent a lot of time there and played with the local kids from the Black community.

Our first authentically Black president, Barak Obama, tells Barkley during his interview for the book, that his entire childhood was spent surrounded by people who looked different from him. Although he describes Hawaii as a particularly tolerant place to grow up, we must remember a white mom and white grandparents raised him. Without a doubt, this exposure helped him to feel more comfortable during times when he was the "only" in a room. This exposure formed the foundation that later developed into what seems his unique ability to feel at ease in any setting. This ease and confidence allowed others to feel at ease in his presence. People opened the doors; people listened; people trusted. No matter our political views, we are all better human beings and Americans for having elected him our president!

Doing this research, it also became apparent that "early and often" is easier and preferable for most when it comes to forming cross-cultural friendships. Later in life may be less probable, and initially less comfortable, but is not at all impossible! The most affirming and inspiring narratives for us, were those we read about Robert F. Kennedy as he travelled the country through much of the sixties. The First, told by Marion Wright Edelman, the civil rights activist and founder of the Children's

Defense Fund:

"I was accompanying Robert Kennedy and his legislative assistant, Peter Edelman, on a tour of the Mississippi Delta, cameras in tow, to show them and the country, the dire conditions of sharecroppers living there. Kennedy decided to enter a shack on his own without the camera crew. I watched undetected while he approached a two-year-old girl on the kitchen floor playing with a piece of rice. He tried for ten minutes to engage this child who couldn't stand and seemed listless from hunger. He finally picked her up, held her in his arms and began rocking her as tears rolled down his face. I knew at that moment he was the real deal. He felt his own children in that moment. I would go on to support his candidacy for president."

Following, are excerpts from his speech on the night Martin

Luther King Jr. was Assassinated on April 4,1968. This speech

was delivered to a mostly Black audience while standing on

the back of a flatbed truck. His aids advised him against

going forward with the planned campaign stop in Indianapolis.

This city is one that experienced no violence on that

hopeless and horrific night. It is widely believed that

Robert Kennedy's words helped this community to grieve

without succumbing to feelings of overwhelming, blinding

anger. He helped this happen by validating that anger.

"For those of you who are black and are tempted to fill with -- be filled with hatred and mistrust of the injustice of such an act, against all white people, I would only say that I also feel in my own heart the same kind of feeling. I had a member of my family killed; killed by a white man. But we have to make an effort in the United States. We have to make an effort to understand, to get beyond, or go beyond these *rather difficult times.*"

This speech marked the first time Bobby Kennedy spoke publicly of his brother Jack's assassination in the five years that had passed since he lost him. The people in this audience felt his empathy, felt his authenticity. He had learned of Dr. Kings' murder only minutes before getting on the back of that truck. The speech was six minutes long. Many scholars consider it his best!

Granted; those in the street on April 4 were looking for answers. Their hearts may have been more open in those moments of internal devastation. Can seemingly simple words or acts of empathy make a difference during the ordinary circumstances of our lives? Research says yes.

Morality and compassion were long regarded as the realm of the religious world. We know now that altruism is part of human evolution. In his work, "The Blank Slate", evolutionary psychologist, Steven Pinker explains, as humans evolved on the African savanna, they had to continually balance two competing needs to survive: taking care of themselves and aiding others. For ten thousand years the emotions associated with those two needs drove our social mores. Pinker writes, "This is why some version of the Golden Rule has appeared in almost all cultures and underlies almost every religion." We read the work of others researching the morality and compassion of human beings using scientific methodology.

Consider the following experiment intended to study the human motivation for kindness conducted by David DeSteno, director of the Social Emotion Group at Northeastern University in Boston. It is described in a fascinating 2012 New York Times article:

"We paired participants in teams; first, they had to tap on sensors to tones played over earphones. In some cases the tones lead the pair to tap in synchrony: in other cases in a mismatched manner. We next had them watch as they're tapping partner got cheated by a person on another team which resulted in the cheated partner being assigned a stack of onerous word problems. As all participants were leaving, they were informed by automated message that if they desired, they could help complete the work assigned to the wronged partner, if they did so, we timed how long they spent at the task. The results were striking. The simple act of tapping ones hand in synchrony with another caused participants to report feeling more similar to their partners and to have greater compassion for their plight: it increased the number of people who helped their partners by 31% and the time they spent helping the partner from one minute to seven minutes. The results suggest that if our minds draw an association between a victim and ourselves-even a relatively trivial one-the compassion we feel for his or her suffering is amplified."

Finding a connection between oneself and another is key. The connection need not be long or meaningful to have some impact on our behavior. These are hopeful findings. Other studies corroborate that small connections matter. We found a couple of great examples worth sharing.

The Journal Science published a study in December 2014 examining attitudes in Los Angeles about same sex marriage. During door to door canvassing half of the canvassers told voters they were gay and why they hoped proposition 8 would pass so that they could have the same benefits of marriage as straight people. The other half offered that they were straight but that they had a friend who they hoped could enjoy the benefits of same sex marriage. A follow up survey one year later revealed a 14 point increase in favorable views of gay marriage from those speaking to a gay canvasser personally and only a 3 point increase in the positive view of those who spoke to a straight individual. The doctoral candidate conducting the study reported being "totally surprised" with the findings and re-ran the experiment fearing the results were incorrect. The results were duplicated the second time around! More than 9,000 voters were included in the experiment. A **single** face-to-face conversation with a gay person advocating for proposition 8 in California changed opinion for the measure dramatically!

We were astounded by another report, this one released by the Joint Commission, a non-profit that provides accreditation to health care organizations, citing doctor/patient communication failure as a primary factor for determining poor patient outcomes:

"Communication failure, rather than a lack of a provider's technical skill, was at the root of at least 70% of serious adverse health outcomes in hospitals"

Lapses in care have a variety of causes. For instance, only about one in four doctors introduce themselves causing patients to forget their physicians name when confused about instructions for home care. On average the doctor listened to patient symptoms for 18 seconds before interrupting them. When observed for the study, it became apparent that many showed a lack of empathy towards patients. One recorded a woman telling her doc of the recent death of a loved one. He answered with: "So how is your abdominal pain?"

Doctors are rushed and can consider empathy and communication skill to be a fluffy extra on their "to do" list. They may reconsider when they learn that giving three minutes of attentive listening to symptoms not only increases health outcomes: it results in fewer malpractice lawsuits against them. Even when a physician was in error, those interviewed for the study reported they would NOT sue a personal doctor they like and feel cares about them! Therefore, evidence shows that it is not only good practice to be empathetic and kind for ones psyche and soul but also for ones business success.

We have witnessed the transformative experience of empathetic listening to someone with a face and a name many times while conducting Diversity classes. The "Fishbowl" unit is particularly powerful in this regard. We do it late in the day once a basic foundation of trust is built. All class-members form a large circle with their chairs. The group is instructed that they will be asked to volunteer to sit in the center three at a time and asked to respond spontaneously and personally to a question asked by the facilitator. The question concerns their individual experience, thus must be answered using a narrative style and with "I" statements without opinion. Those on the outside of this three-person "fishbowl" just watch and listen, but cannot interact with the center group. The questions change with each new center group. Here are a few examples of the sort of questions:

"Talk about an early experience in which you felt culturally different from others around you and it was not a good feeling."

"Talk about a stereotype from your cultural group that makes you feel proud and one that makes you feel uncomfortable."

"Tell a story about a time when you overcame a cultural barrier to communication with someone."

It is always amazing for us to witness just how quickly a thirty year old recalls a hurtful incident from the first grade as if it happened yesterday. The stories

are honest and authentic. The differences being described

by individuals in the circle seem somehow to be relatable

to everyone no matter which childhood experience of

feeling uncomfortably different is being described. Nobody

present during this fishbowl story needed to have lived on

a farm in rural Mexico to feel Juan's pain as he spoke:

"We were living on a farm in the middle of nowhere. I
guess we were poor, but I didn't know it. I helped my
parents, played with my siblings, rode donkeys and ate
fresh food. One day my father told us we had to leave for
the city. He wanted his children to have schooling and
that was the only place to get it. His word was law. We
left our world. Everything was different. My parents were
so proud to send me off with my new pants and short
carefully combed hair to my first day of school. I will
never forget that first humiliating day. I ran all the way
home crying. The other kids were laughing and yelling
"huaraches rapidos, huaraches rapidos!" as they pointed at
my feet! They were chanting "speedy sandals, speedy
sandals!" My parents didn't know that only country
bumpkins wore sandals with tire rubber on the soles. My
pappy found me some shoes. They sacrificed a lot for us."

These heartfelt tales of exclusion frequently center on

ethnic difference, but not always. One young woman

recanted her embarrassment when she was required to sell

giftwrap for her elementary school. Even if she managed to

find someone to pay $10.00 for a role of fancy paper, how

could they get it sent to them? Everybody her family knew

had only a small mail slot on the wall next to all the

other mail slots. Her neighbors didn't have houses at

which a large package could be left. There was no doorman

or building manager to sign for it. It could be taken by any number of vagrants or teenagers crowding the entry to her unlocked apartment building. She recalled her feeling of shame when she found any number of excuses for failing to bring the order sheet back to school. Most of the other kids in her third grade class had filled the order page with the names of neighbors and co-workers cornered by parents in the high rise offices where they worked. Her mom cleaned office buildings in the middle of the night. Her dad worked fixing roofs with an uncle when needed.

George told the circle of his experience starting a new school in the fourth grade during the early 70's. When he told the other kids his move was the result of his parent's divorce, they gasped in shock. He was a specimen, the first kid with a working, divorced and single mother in his class. Birthday Party invites became scarce!

During another memorable fishbowl, an upbeat and animated first year school nurse was struggling. "I can't really think of one; come back to me." When we did come back around to Sangeeta, she remembered something. This smiling woman, so proud of choosing a career caring for others, told us about her memories of "feeling different" during her first post-college job in India. She had grown up in a far southern district where she and most other residents had darker skin than their northern counterparts. Her first job in nursing took her to a northern province where her skin was noticeably darker than her colleagues at the hospital. Sangeeta told of having to frequently convince perplexed looking doctors and nurses that she was, in fact, a nurse educated and qualified for this position. Initially, most assumed this dark skinned nurse was a cleaning woman. She was routinely asked to do up a bed or take care of a bathroom. When told she was a nurse, Sangeeta tried to ignore the puzzled looks on the faces of Doctors in the hospital. Her colleagues had formed a mental picture of a nurse in their minds and she just didn't fit the stereotype.

This occurred on the other side of the world, yet her story resonated so strongly that the next person to share her tale of "otherness" had a remarkably similar experience to share. Anna's darker skin tone also confused others in certain settings. Curiously, this confusion commonly occurred in the laundry room of her apartment building. More than once, a neighbor seeking conversation asked Anna whose apartment she was cleaning. The neighbors had a mental picture that dark and Spanish speaking equaled housekeeper. This is similar to the familiar instances of Brown and Black men becoming magnets for car keys in the valet parking area. Having an automatic visual association between parking attendant and Latino in Los Angeles is not an image concocted out of thin air. The two may fit together in your mind due to past encounters. Does the thought make you an ignorant bigot? We argue it does not. However, assuming you know the identity of another based on past encounters, is not wise or thoughtful. In fact, even if the last 22 of 24 valet parking attendants that crossed your path were of Central American heritage, you shouldn't assume the next person standing in front of a restaurant sporting a white shirt with dark hair and skin, is waiting for your car keys!

White folks may imagine these cases of mistaken identity ought to be understandable to the person of color. "What's the big deal?" they may think. "It's just an innocent mistake." It would be wise to consider that the "servant" label has likely been placed on the person with whom you made "the little mistake" before, many times before! They are tired of it. Use empathy, not statistics!

The fishbowl format allows our white participants a chance to express pain and discomfort also. The assignment calls for revealing a personal story of feeling uncomfortable and shamed by ones own difference, any apparent difference, during a specific and describable time and place.

For the majority of "cultural sensitivity" programs the two of us have attended, we have observed the white participants express one of two emotions. The first, and most common, are feelings of guilt for the history of race discrimination in America perpetrated by whites and for the privilege this discrimination has afforded them societally. The second group consists of white individuals expressing resentment for being labeled the oppressor. These folks may even feel themselves the victims of what they consider reverse racism. During either of these scenarios, white attendees say little while in mixed company. We see lots of heads nodding in agreement from the "guilt" contingent while they listen intently to speakers of color. In the other group, the resentful one, heads are bent over their barely hidden I-phone screens or they keep busy engaging like-minded friends in the universally understood, sarcastic eye roll.

In our experience, simply creating a space allowing white students to share a personally painful "culture-based" story, ends up creating a more authentic and unifying experience for all. It is important to expand the typical definition of a cultural group.

Being part of a culture is to be associated with a stereotypical set of beliefs and behaviors by others because of your physical appearance, your place of current residence or place of origin, your education and profession and the others with whom you choose to spend time with socially. The author, Jeff Chang, wrote a definition of culture we find flawless.

"Culture is the realm of images, ideas, sounds and stories. It is our shared space. It is the narrative we are immersed in everyday. It is where people find community and express our values."

Expanding our definition of culture in a way that reaches beyond race, allows for the possibility of building empathy for others we previously saw as "un-relatable". For example, in class, a white woman reveals the pain she felt when school friends asked her if she had a "real mom" upon discovering that Patricia was adopted. Others come to understand her adopted status placed her in a kind of culture. Patricia feels a sense of sympathy from others for the discomfort this caused her as a child. She senses that she is now being seen as more than her "white privileged" status.

A black participant, following Patricia's story, may talk about a childhood memory in which a white child called her skin "dirty", or a more recent indignity she felt when asked by a white co-worker "How did you get this job?" A light bulb turns on for those participants who believed that racism no longer exists because we have a black president and first family.

Stories of everyday indignities illuminate the consciousness of the more privileged majority. "Wow, these black and brown folks have experienced demeaning experiences on a daily basis, yet are willing to validate pain I feel as a member of a culture easily hidden at will. It's true, white privilege does exist. I live in a world where I enjoy race based privileges I never considered, and I ought to acknowledge them!"

Another of our most impactful workshop activities brings about particularly strong empathetic response from nearly everyone in attendance. We call it The Cultural Object Presentation. The group is instructed to return on Day Two of the seminar with an object that represents the culture they most identify themselves with. It is basically an old-fashioned show and tell circle! By this juncture in the class, we hope that those who previously described themselves as "without a culture" have caught on that we all have multiple cultural identities. These come from ones family history and beliefs but can also stem from any group with whom we share powerful common experiences and attitudes about our world.

Some of the cultural object presentations are surprising and offer food for thought! For instance, a woman once brought a bottle of vodka and her sobriety chip as her cultural object. She was able to convincingly share the important role drinking alcohol had played in her life and in the lives of many of her family and friends. The bottle was always present. It wasn't a holiday or a celebration without it. Becoming sober immersed her in an entirely new and foreign cultural group. Ellen painfully described the loss of her old culture as she attempted to join a new one. Many of the people and places of comfort and familiarity were gone. She needed a new language and different surroundings. Being sober meant giving up a large and familiar piece of her identity. In fact, she felt so strongly about her need to describe her alcoholism as a culture, that bringing this cultural object to the presentation had been her first time actually touching a vodka bottle in five years!

We have witnessed cultural presentations of all sorts. Ancestral cultures are the most prominent and run deep. Objects have included such items as a front door key from a home abandoned by her family while fleeing the Armenian genocide of 1915, to a set of long white paper gloves and a face mask sent from her native Korea, a gift from a mother to her daughter in Los Angeles, so that her skin doesn't darken while driving on a sunny day. We learned many Korean women wear them because light skin is considered a desired standard of beauty.

We are in agreement that the most memorable of the cultural objects ever presented was the one brought by a young teacher, James. He arrived to the morning circle with a black boom box sort of cassette player. Other participants were settling in to their seats placing the more typical photo albums, baby clothing, athletic wear, books or plates of special food on their laps. When it was his turn, James didn't introduce his object by describing it the way most participants do; instead he put the player down beside him and hit play. He said nothing. We listened to a beautiful voice singing *"O Holy Night"* When the song ended, James stopped the tape and told us that the lovely soprano voice on the machine had been his before his transition from female to male. He explained that singing with the choir had been a very important part of his identity, his culture, for his young life. When taking the hormones he needed to transition into the man he was on the inside, he had lost that voice. In fact, James could no longer sing. On hearing this, not a soul in our circle of mostly mainstream, heterosexual, suburban strangers registered even a fleeting look of shock or disapproval. It was quite remarkable to witness! This was the second day of the training. The group had spent the first day building trust while sharing increasingly personal information. Everybody had a face and a name at this juncture. The stereotypes had taken a backseat for this extraordinary moment.

The hope for us as facilitators is that these flickers of empathetic understanding for the "different" of society will continue to spark in the world outside of this manufactured and temporary cocoon. We hope the experience causes us to question our automatic biases when they inevitably arise.

It helps for all of us to pause and consider the wise and powerful words of Atticus Finch, the iconic heroine of Harper Lee's American classic, *"To Kill a Mockingbird"*, as he tucked his young daughter Scout into bed for the night. His advice holds the key to developing empathy.

"You never really understand a person until you consider things from his point of view, Climb inside his skin and walk around in it a while"

Unfortunately, in this world, we rarely get the chance to engage in any sort of empathetic discussion with those who's lives differ markedly from our own, let alone get the chance to gather a basic understanding of what it

would be like to "Walk around in their skin awhile".
Those that take part in our hours long, professionally
facilitated discussion focused on developing empathy and
communication skill, as the by-product of learning to
understand others, are paid to be there! How might we as a
community develop the important and illusive ability
displayed by Atticus Finch? Is it even possible " To
consider things from another's point of view?" *We whole-
heartedly believe it is possible. However, It ain't easy*

Join Us

Many "well meaning" Americans profess to disregard color in their relations with other people. "Aren't we all the same on the inside?" is the mantra of "non-racist" among us. Deborah Plummer, author and diversity consultant, explains the pitfalls of this "color-blind" approach in her book *"Racing Across the Lines-Changing Race Relations Through Friendship"*:

"The "color-blind" approach is one of the many ways we have handled our racial differences, and it has been considered by many to be forward thinking because it de-emphasizes racial differences and emphasizes racial similarities. In theory, it appears to be affirming diversity, but in practice it can demonstrate a hierarchical and patronizing approach. In other words, in order for me as a white American to deal with you as a person of color, I have to pretend that I only see the ways in which we are the same. In reality, I see that you are a person of color but relate to you as if you were just like me. I realize there are many well-intentioned individuals who believe that being color-blind is a way to erase difference but differences cannot be erased any more than I can bring the dead back to life."

There are many studies confirming that indeed, most whites choose to demonstrate their preferred "color-blind" view of race by practicing stony silence on the topic. Two of the books we read cited particularly enlightening

examples of this popular attitude. In his 2014 book, "Who
We Be…The Colorization of America", Jeff Chang, references
a Vanderbilt University study in which %75 of white
parents admit they do not speak to their children about
race. He also reports that when Millennia's' where asked
the question "Do you feel comfortable having a discussion
on racial bias?" 80% say they are not comfortable. These
are the very same enlightened young people that believe
the age of post racial America has arrived. The other
study, cited in "Nurture Shock", an acclaimed parenting
book written by Po Bronson and Ashley Merryman, includes
an eye-opening chapter with the title: "Why White Parents
Don't Talk About Race"

The chapter begins with the story of a University of
Texas study conducted to determine the effect, if any, of
watching multiculturally themed children's videos on young
children's racial attitudes. The Ph.D. graduate students
recruited 100 local Caucasian families with young children
to participate. After watching the videos, parents were
told to start a conversation with their children about
some of the themes presented. It was suggested that
parents ask the children "jumping off" questions such as
whether they thought it would be nice to have a Black or
Mexican child as a friend or if kids from other

backgrounds liked the same things they liked. The families were to engage in this way for five nights and the parents were to write about the discussions on a provided form.

The study authors administered the Racial Attitude Measure questionnaire to the 5-7 year old students separately both before and after the video and discussion assignment. The Ph.D. thesis students were disappointed to find a greatly improved racial attitude in only six of the one hundred participants. Follow-up investigation revealed the reason. The six were the children of the parents reporting having had in depth, meaningful discussions on race after viewing the videos! The rest of the parent diaries revealed a mention of a phrase like "everybody's equal" after watching, but included no feedback from further in depth discussion. When presses as to why this section of the diary was sparse, the majority expressed discomfort with how to talk about skin color difference in addition to having fear of what their children might say.

The parents were correct to fear what their kindergarten student might say about race difference. They live in a zone filled with "We are all the same" talk! The Bronson and Merryman book contains clues as to contents of such long avoided conversation. It turns out children are generally attracted to other children that look like them.

This developmentally normal preference for the physically similar has a scientific name, essentialism. When asked, kids will assign positive attributes such as beauty, brains and kindness to those who look most like them. The preference may be based on gender, size or skin color, but children will choose their "in group" based on what "like me" attributes they see in front of them. The good news is that we are apparently wired to search for empathetic connection. The bad news is that we assume an empathetic relationship will come only from those that seem familiar from the outset. The mind says "It looks like me, talks like me and dresses like me. It must like what I like."

Certainly, empathy is statistically more likely to occur when two seem similar at first glance, but can and does happen, with unlikely groupings. We see this often in our workshops. We do our best to be the catalysts for lowering typical boundaries to authentic communication. You too, can probably rattle off examples of unlikely buddies that have developed without having begun the friendship at a cultural diversity seminar. There are times in life when the dream of Atticus Finch, that one may climb inside another's skin and walk around for a while, are achievable. For us, the key piece of advice we take from the wise hero of "To Kill a Mockingbird" is the phrase "a while". No one can possibly crawl in to the skin of another completely or forever. Personally, we wouldn't want to! We find assimilation boring! The goal for us is acculturation. With acculturation, one can "cross borders" comfortably but need not give up unique cultural characteristics they enjoy sharing with others.

Charles Barkley, NBA star and contemporary philosopher, speaks to this distinction in his book "Who's Afraid of a Large Black Man" He reminds the reader that people utilize different sorts of speech patterns and vocabulary when talking with an elder, with a member of the clergy or with their golf buddies. Nothing is wrong with using different communication styles with people in different cultural settings? It doesn't make a person inauthentic or a "wanna be", the term used colloquially to label anyone who doesn't tow the cultural line prescribed.

Lots of folks express interest in developing a connection with the "other" sharing common space with them. However, for those in the minority, it often seems that assimilation to the majority or cultural preservation through separation are the only available choices. Consider the words of this young man attending what he describes as an elite private high school in L.A.

"Everything about my classmates was so new, that when faced with the decision to assimilate on campus, or maintain my identity, I didn't have a choice. I just wouldn't feel comfortable pretending I love football or basketball or that I care about which bands are playing at Coachella. We only ever talk about soccer in Lennox, and our Coachella consists of backyard concerts. But even if I am still a Mexican kid on campus, it doesn't mean I only want to hang out with students of color. There are some amazing people at this school who I'd love to get to know better. I just don't feel I can be their friend without loosing who I am. It doesn't have to be that way. Ultimately, the student body has to take responsibility for this change, even if it means stepping outside our comfort zones and beyond our own zip codes."

He sincerely wishes to expand his friend group and challenges other students on campus to get out of their comfort zones in this brave op-ed piece printed in the March 2013 issue of Crossfire, the Crossroads School student run magazine. He seems to wonder whether acculturation, though desirable, is possible.

One need simply watch a few culturally based comedy shows on television to get a sense of the daily difficulties involved in trying to navigating life in a majority white setting while simultaneously trying to maintain a separate cultural identity. Our favorites from the genre are Chris Rock and Ali Leroy of "Everybody Hates Chris" airing 2005-2009, Eddie Huang of "Fresh Off the Boat" 2015 and Anthony Anderson of "Blackish" also premiering 2015.

The scenarios are plentiful and hilarious! In the semi-autobiographical sitcom "Everybody Hates Chris", Chris is a kid from the majority black and working class neighborhood, Bedford Stuyvesant, in New York City sent to a majority white school on the other side of town by his parents who believe the educational opportunities are superior to his local school. At the school he is alternately shown being perceived by his white classmates and teachers as either a tough thug who causes hallways to empty and classroom doors to slam for no reason every time he appears or as a charity case to be pitied. There are web sites focused solely on the "well meaning" but racist comments made by the character depicting the stereotypical *"white savior " type teacher*, Ms. Morello.

In one episode, the class is told they must sell cookies to family and neighbors in order to raise money for a class field trip. Ms. Morello approaches Chris beaming her exaggerated, caring, smile as she stops at his desk, looks down into his eyes in front of the entire class, and tells him "ever so kindly"; "You don't have to sell any cookies Chris. I know people in your neighborhood don't have any cash." Following the offer, her face lights up with a "Why didn't I think of that!" look. Ms. Morello announces her "great idea"! "Chris, I am going to try to arrange it so that we can accept food stamps for these cookies. Then you can sell them to your people. Isn't that a wonderful idea, Chris?" she blurts out. Chris isn't able to protest, of course! This woman means well and is just *soooo* nice to him in front of the rest of the class, he doesn't want to appear rude to her. The scene is so artfully acted that the viewer literally feels this kids embarrassment while his classmates remain oblivious to the insult. The "knowing" white viewer gains the ability to hear themselves in this teacher's inappropriate, but "nice", remarks to Chris. The "patronizing white savior" archetype is exaggerated for comic effect, but the kernel of truth is unmistakable; good intentions don't replace awareness!

In another comical "living among whites" situation airing on the sitcom "Blackish", Andre's biracial wife Rainbow, becomes concerned that her flabby husband will be injured if he continues to play basketball with his current group of guys. She pleads with him:

"Dre, I want you to start playing ball with guys named Colin and Ethan from now on! No more Malik's and Jamal's for you! He scrunches up his face in disgust. "You want me to play with whites?" he whines to his wife Rainbow

How is it that Andre immediately knows Ethan and Colin are shorthand references for "white guys who are not big and tough?" Does he have special powers? NOPE. He knows it in the same way we know it! These names have a strong association in American minds. The joke works because of the stereotype associated with these names.

Finally, the third common white stereotype worth noting is the one depicted brilliantly in an episode of "Fresh Off the Boat" titled "Phillip Goldstein". In this one, the school principal asks Eddie Huang, the main character and only Asian kid in his Orlando, Florida middle school, to befriend the new kid, Philip Goldstein. He is the new kid with Asian features and white Jewish adoptive parents, the Goldstein's. Eddie bluntly asks whether the request came his way because Philip is Asian, and therefore, needs an Asian buddy? The principal gasps with shock and surprise at Eddie's question. "I hadn't noticed he was Chinese", is his embarrassed reply.

Basically, white folks tend to be stereotyped as "deer in the headlights" scared, overly and insincerely nice, physically weak or laughably blind to difference, when interacting with people of color. The irony, of course, is that it is the avowed non-racists who fall into these categories most often. Consider this internal monologue shared in the GQ magazine article, "Will You Be My Black Friend", by Devin Friedman, while he was glancing nervously around the room at a party at which he was the only white guy present.

"It's hard enough to be at a party where you don't know anyone. But when you are the only white guy, you feel like you can't even be awkward in private. And when do you talk to someone, there's a social hump between you. It's like you are having two conversations, the actual conversation and the subtitled one, which goes: You are black. You are white. Hello black person! Hello white person!"

Friedman is having this frenetic exchange in his head because he so wants to be seen as a non-racist that he doesn't know what to say! The nervous energy began long before Friedman entered the room. While getting ready for the party, he asked his wife not to dress like "a tomboy", because "Black folks don't dress like that." She reminded him that she would still be white whether she wore the "right shoes" or not! Friedman revealed his wife also chided him for thanking the black guy who, while standing on a corner in Harlem, gave him a Jesus Saves flyer, "If that guy were white, You'd never have taken that."

This uncomfortable, invisible "force-field of doubt" Friedman describes surrounding him, is not imaginary, but neither is his sincere desire for increased understanding and easy conversation. We believe Mr. Friedman is not alone in his interest or in his trepidation. Fortunately, there are individuals who share in his desire for better communication between disparate communities, who also have the powerful voice and substantial resources necessary to spread the message to the rest of us.

The two of us joined everyone else in the country in witnessing the most public and far-reaching effort to "Get us talking" ever attempted by one of these powerful, influential and respected voices of the liberal elite! In March 2015, Howard Shultz, CEO of Starbucks, requested that thousands of his employees voluntarily write the words "Race Together" on coffee cups next to the name and drink preference of their customer. The words were intended as an invitation to the customer interested in opening a discussion, or asking a question, related to the usually taboo topic of race relations.

If you have television, radio, newspaper or internet service, you know the nationwide roll-out of the "Race Together" campaign was greeted with a backlash from customers and pundits alike we can only describe as swift and deafening! Social media exploded with replies to this effort from Shultz. Representative samples include:

The angry: "I don't have time to describe 400 years of oppression to you, and make my train"

The sarcastic: "I think people of color who work at Starbucks confronting white people about race/class as they pay six dollars for a latte seems great."

The absurd and funny: "By any beans necessary" and "I have a cream"

In fact, Starbucks Senior Vice President for Global Communications, Corey DeBrowa, reported temporarily deleting his twitter account because: "The Cascade of negativity felt like a personal attack."

Larry Wilmore, host of the Daily Show with Larry Wilmore, provided the commentary on the "Race Together" debacle, which resonated most with us. He addressed his audience on the March 29 broadcast of his show with passion and conviction:

"Starbucks wasn't blasted for having a conversation about race, they were blasted for wanting to have a conversation about race. That's how much we need to have a conversation about race. We can't even talk about talking about it!"

We agree! Thoughtful people ought to be able to engage in meaningful conversations about difficult topics. The problem with having these conversations, is that few are able to take the first, and most important, step needed in order to engage in meaningful dialogue:

LISTEN TO THE OTHER PERSON!

You may be thinking, "That's too simplistic, of course I listen." Maybe you do, most don't do it well. It takes great focus. We consider the translated meaning of the Chinese word for "listen" to be an excellent barometer. The Ting character, the one for listen, consists of joining the individual symbols for ears, eyes, undivided attention and heart. This offers a powerful and necessary combination for listening in any language!

How does it look and sound to us when another is listening with their ears, eyes and heart? How do we recognize the difference between a true question and an assumption wrapped in the disguise of a question? First, we'll share personal examples of this common mistake.

Kari: Nearly every time I tell someone I am Jewish and from Boston, they ask; "So, are you from Newton or Wellesley?" They never ask, "What part of Boston are you from?" People seem compelled to make me aware that they are *"in the know"* when it comes to Jewish suburbs. I love seeing their faces when I tell them, "Actually, no, I'm from the *"Not Newton"* contingent; you know, the folks from the wrong side of the Boston Jewish tracks!

La Fonda: When married acquaintances discover I am a single parent, the question is always the same; " How do you handle being both mother and father to your son? Aren't you worried about how hard it is for Morgan without a male teaching him man things?

Both remarks have question marks on the end. Then they are questions, "aren't they?" To the one listening to the *"question"*, there is no difficulty discerning the difference between curiosity and opinion. The *"asker"* just can't seem to get their opinion out of the question. This person may not even have the ability to distinguish between the question; "How has it been for you as a single parent?" and the non-question: "Isn't it difficult to being a single mom? Is your child acting up because he doesn't have a dad?" The answer is often delivered in a defensive or dismissive manner. The *"asker"* is then left wondering why their *"sincere"* show of concern is not welcome by the askee! Discomfort ensues.

One of our workshop units begins with, "Does anyone remember the don't ask, don't tell controversy regarding gays in the military?" They do. We tell them this particular unit is based on our twist on the phrase. We call it "ask, don't tell". The class is then divided into groups of five. They walk around the room together pausing at each of six newsprints hung on the walls. On each is a phrase written as a question, but is actually a statement. For example, we post "How can you possibly take care of six children on your salary?" and "Isn't your long commute a nightmare?" Other favorites include the often angering, "What are you, where are you from?" or "Was it really confusing for you to grow up with two dads?" Finally, we might post "Have you met your child's real mom?" or "Is your neighborhood dangerous at night?"

Each group must work together constructing phrases that turn the "tells" written on the newsprint into true "asks". The task calls for removing the embedded assumptions in front of them. When complete, we hope to see a variety of actual questions replacing the original statements framed as questions, and discuss their group process and it's importance for them.

Turning *"tells"* into *"asks"* takes practice. The flash of annoyance on the part of the "askee" when confronted with these statements confuses and frightens the "asker". "Who needs this?" both simultaneously think to themselves, while walking away from the stressful exchange.

We thought it helpful to construct a list of some of the "tells" most often presented as "asks". These comments have been repeatedly described to us as being particularly insensitive and annoying to an "askee". First, read our underlined description of an "askee" stereotypically offended by an unknowing or uncaring "asker". Below the description, read the offending "tell" disguised as an "ask" on the left side of the page, and our version of the same phrase reworked into an authentic "ask" on the right side. There is a difference!

An African American boy in basketball shorts.

TELL: What do you play, center?	ASK: What do you like to do after school?

A new female employee

TELL: "Do you have a boyfriend?"	ASK: "Are you dating someone special?"

An African American couple at a dinner party

TELL: ASK:
"Which black revival church   "Do you belong to a
  do you belong to?"   religious institution?"

A woman with a skin color different than her child

TELL: ASK:
"Whose baby is that?"   "Are you having fun with
                          your little cutie pie?"

Now that you are beginning to master the skill of asking and not telling in the same breath, lets learn about a few more requirements of successfully engaging in cross-cultural communication:

ACCEPTANCE DOES NOT MEAN AGREEMENT:

Again, as with listening, you may be telling yourself, "I accept everyone!" The typical, self-described liberals in this country are quick to describe themselves as especially tolerant and accepting of difference. They are sincere in this belief. It is the definition of difference that can be fraught with difficulty. Usually, a professed open minded, non-judgmental liberal is more than willing to accept difference in skin color, difference in membership in a *mainstream* religion or family lifestyle, a different sexual orientation or career choice. It becomes far more difficult to "accept difference" when it means accepting another parent's discipline and extra-curricula choices for their children, their drug and alcohol use or feelings about schooling, the value they place on medicine or in their choice of a religion that restricts certain types of clothing, requires women to wear head coverings or that forbid the use of birth control for adherents. Acceptance takes fortitude and an internal mantra-like reminder that acceptance is not agreement. We don't have to like it, but if we want or need to communicate with the stranger we have deemed *strange*, we must lean toward acceptance!

Some believe and behave in ways that many of us find abhorrent. However, at times, we must interact with, and show concern for, individuals we disagree with the most. For example, decent public school teachers, employers, mentors, and yes, us cultural diversity consultants, have a mandate to accept while disagreeing or disliking. We find this pill goes down more easily when we try to understand the origin or reasons for a belief or behavior.

For instance, Kari shares a story illustrating the dilemma. She heard some of her Iranian and Israeli raised neighbors hide cash income so that their children may qualify for private school and college scholarships. She says it is widely known in her community that some of these families consider it acceptable to lie about their home address in order that their children can attend public school in the Beverly Hills school district. This bothered her. She complains they shouldn't ask for money while driving fancy cars and building pools in their back yard. "Where are their morals? Is this what they teach their children?" she wonders aloud. It bothers her that many Persian's and Israeli's in Los Angeles are stereotyped as being unconcerned about the community beyond their own, as being pushy and materialistic and fears this may reflect on her as a Jew.

We discussed our judgments. We "knew" our spending choices were superior to those "show-offs" in both of our cultures of origin." Weren't they just plain crass, nouveau rich Jews or Bougie Black folks, when their behavior was distasteful to us? We challenged ourselves to dig deeper, to look for the why, to look for the lessons to be learned from these strange strangers. We learned that in some communities where money is scarce, spending extravagantly and visibly is the way to celebrate a success that might disappear tomorrow. It is frequently the way in which one receives the status and respect long denied them. We learned that for some, adherence to the philosophy "survival of the fittest" is the *only* choice. One must bribe, barter and "put one over" to do almost anything. A system we dislike has worked for them for generations.

Aren't these the very same people who invite us for elaborate meals with no expectation of reciprocation? Don't they throw their keys at us when they leave town begging, "Use the pool, eat the food, enjoy!" Everyone is invited, ALWAYS. Kari once mentioned to an Israeli born friend that her parents would be staying at a hotel when they arrived. This typically friendly and talkative neighbor was frozen, speechless and shocked, upon hearing the news; then she began to yell:

"How can you not have them in your house! Make a bed for them, Cook meals for them? Aghh, cold heartless Americans! My parents come for at least a month and it's beautiful! Do your parents even know your daughter? Unbelievable!"

Basically, Kari's behavior is seen as *"cold"* and *"strange"* by her neighbor. It is unthinkable to the woman that Kari would put her family out of her house. Hmmm...seeing things from the other person's point of view. It certainly isn't easy, but it may help you learn to search for reasons why and then to accept!

OUR WAY IS NOT THE ONLY WAY:

With time and reflection, we may develop the capacity
to accept certain unappealing behaviors from people of a
different cultural viewpoint; the spending habits, the
conversational styles, the eating and socializing styles,
even those "crazy" opinions vociferously aired to all in
ear shot! But can we possibly accept cultural practices we
consider abusive, or ones that seem to us, to be steeped
in a sort of cultural self-hatred practiced unconsciously
by the individual from another group? This is a tall
order, especially for white liberals.

For instance, Eddie Huang, author of "Fresh off the
Boat" publicly shared his anger about the way in which he
felt his book, and subsequently his life experience, was
being "sanitized" for the American television audience
when it's contents became the basis for a sitcom of the
same title. For him, to leave out childhood episodes of
family life that included physical punishment was to
disregard his parent's long held cultural beliefs
regarding the best methods of reward and discipline needed
to raise successful children.

Every Friday afternoon, Huang says, social workers
would take him out of class to inspect him for bruises. He
says he "was made to feel he was weird, like there was

something wrong with us." He credits his parents stern, culturally based methods, including being made to kneel in his driveway for hours as a punishment for stealing, with making him into the success he is today.

In fact, he vividly remembers the first time he didn't feel weirdly different from the white kids. He recounts a trip to the grocery store with his mom. This was the place where he saw the parents of mid-eastern and black children slap their kids for the same things he was slapped for in a store, touching stuff or bruising fruit. In the same grocery, he recalled that the white kids literally threw fruit across the store while their docile mom gently asked them to: "Please walk away or please behave". He describes these encounters as early lessons in racial difference as well as the beginning of his interest in, and kinship with, black culture.

Confession, We are moms that came up in the age of time out and "talking" about consequences to our kids. We found these methods worked just fine for us. We were taught violence and fear creates violence and fear, that our parent's methods were wrong and harmful. Are we too soft?

"Eddie, don't worry, sanitized or not, we were shocked by some of the scenes chosen to depict the behavior of your Chinese mom! We wish you were there to see us after the episode when mom wouldn't put the little guy's school-work on the fridge until it was perfect. We looked at each other the way we would if we suddenly saw a beautiful bleeding puppy on the street, hands to heart, big sad eyes and a chorus of Oh my God! We asked our friend Shawn if he had seen it. He replied, "I usually think that show is so funny, but I swear I am still having nightmares about the refrigerator scene!"

But hasn't corporal punishment been proven damaging? Must we accept it as valid cultural practice? It turns out, yes *and* no! Consider the following results from the Kenneth Dodge K-12 longitudinal study of the effect of physical punishment on over 400 black and white children cited in the book "Nurture Shock":

"In the white community Dodge studied, physical discipline was a mostly unspoken taboo. It was saved only for the *worst offenses*. The parent was usually very angry at the child and had lost his or her temper. The implicit message was: What you have done is so deviant that you deserve a special punishment, spanking. It marked the child as someone who had lost his place within traditional society. These kids became more aggressive. In the black community, where physical punishment occurred only slightly more than in the white community studied, it was conveyed as normal and had no negative effect on these kids aggression over the years."

It's not just a Black or White thing:

"A University of Texas study, also cited in the book, examined the effects of physical punishment in a conservative white protestant community. One-third of the respondents from this community spanked their kids three or more times per week. The study found no negative effects in the children of this group either,---precisely because spanking was conveyed to children as normal."

Both studies found that it was the attitude and actions of the parent doing the spanking, and how they described the need for spanking to their child during the episode, that made the difference. If spanking was the "thing to do" when a kid misbehaved, it normalized the practice. If spanking was described as for the "horrible and uncontrollable" child who "drove me to evil", negative and violent behaviors more commonly resulted from that child.

Those of us on the *"educated-liberal"* team, also harbor strong opinions about the ways in which members of other peoples cultures ought to speak to each other, wear their hair and clothing, or view their facial features and skin tone. Us members of the enlightened class just *know* when someone of color is being exploited by mainstream white or conservative religious propaganda, don't we?

It's complicated. A couple of years ago a teacher originally from the Philippines, brought her whitening cream to class as her cultural object. She described this cream as an important part of her identity as a Pilipino woman. She said everyone used it, it was prominently advertised on her local billboards, and reminded her warmly of her home culture. Of course, all of listened intently and did not judge her choice of cultural object. However, as facilitators of future seminars, we recalled the story as a sad and cautionary tale of the power of colonialism and Caucasian standards of beauty.

About six months later, a Korean born teacher brought a white linen mask and a set of fingerless gloves reaching above her elbows to share as her cultural object. She explained the items were a staple for Korean women and were designed to keep the skin from getting dark when driving. This time, anticipating a backlash for "wanting to be white", she told the group others had criticized her for using this stuff, but that she has a right to follow the cultural norms she chooses. Is it the duty or responsibility for those of us in the teeth straightening, hair coloring, eyebrow plucking, and freckle removing community, to tell another they are a bamboozled self-hater "wanna-bees"; maybe not. Just a thought!

Aren't there any universal values or beliefs? What about standards and norms of behavior? This is a delicate area, but can be addressed more easily than you think. In fact, our description of the "norms" is more important than the norms themselves.

The public educational setting is likely the largest system we have developed to encourage, and ultimately enforce, behavioral norms for young Americans. In our capacity as continuing education facilitators, we have the advantage of working with teachers from all over Los Angeles county in a setting in which we have no "paycheck power" over the participants. That is, we feel our setting is one in which truth emerges more easily than in a setting in which spoken truth can bring real consequence to a classroom teacher. The "truths" we hear are filled with teacher frustration at students and parents they believe do not value them or the lessons they teach.

We use the two most important messages of the training, "ask, don't tell" and "acceptance is not agreement" to help them address the frustration. The words used, and the tone conveyed, do matter! We begin this unit with a role-play in which the teachers act out a difficult exchange experienced with a parent or student at school. The role- play allows the teachers to feel heard, while simultaneously allowing us to listen to the language and attitude being portrayed as those of the teacher, the student, or the parent, in a given scenario. We "unpack" the scene with the input of the other teachers. As you might imagine, the scenes begin with "Johnny is doing badly in my class, he doesn't bring his homework" or to the child "You are so disrespectful! Do your parents let you act so badly at home?" The parent may reply; "You are always picking on my child, you don't help him." The child might stare at the window or tell you "Just send me to the principals office."

We help the "actors" to reframe the wording without loosing the message. With the help of other participants, we brainstorm suggestions. Maybe we advise starting a parent conference by asking "Can you give me one example of a way in which Johnny matured this year? Followed by the question "Can you tell one way in which Johnny frustrates you at home? Is there any one thing that you hope Johnny learns this year? Lets talk about ways we could make that happen for him."

We do not want to give the impression that the hurdles faced by underachieving schools in low-income neighborhoods, are easily overcome; instead, we want to convey the power of respect on relationship. Using the "ask" method does convey respect, precisely because it is so rare an experience for many, especially the young. The "ask" is one tool, acceptance is another. When you take a moment to explain to a child that the expectations you set for the classroom are *DIFFERENT, but not necessarily BETTER than the expectations set elsewhere, you are taking the shame out of the equation.* You are telling the child that you believe they have the ability to adjust to different situations; that making these distinctions means they are smart! It is a message that conveys knowledge and acceptance on the part of the teacher that various behaviors and beliefs exist in different settings, often with a reason, but cannot exist in this setting. Your reason ought to be explained, not assumed.

In addition to developing enhanced communication in the teacher-student and teacher-parent relationship, the classroom holds great possibility for creating respect and communication *BETWEEN* students. This is an all too frequently missed opportunity. For sure, during our seminar, teachers tell us they do wish students weren't so separated by ethnic group in class and on the playground. For teachers in the upper grades, the complaint goes beyond student disinterest in the other; it becomes student dislike and antagonism toward the other.

Mostly, these teachers express feeling helpless in their ability to create any sort of friendship between groups, and are busy simply "keeping the peace."

We tell them that we are convinced that classroom teachers have more power to create community than any other authority figure in society. Our claim brings the following typical pushback:

"But, I'm nice to everyone. I always tell the kids to stop saying disrespectful things to each other. I explain that we fought to end segregation and staying separate is what the racists want you to do."

We have no doubt the desire is there, as is the heart!

We listen to the frustrated comments from the educators before asking, "Do you assign work projects or take field trips and allow your students to pick their own partners?" The answers are usually similar:

"Yes, my students enjoy working with friends on projects. As a treat for good behavior, I let them arrange their desks into table groups of their choice. Sometimes I ask them to pair up with someone they don't know well for a field trip, but they seem to end up walking around with friends anyway."

We gently inform the teachers that they have been ignoring a fantastic opportunity to build community, and we can prove it! Now it's time to remind these grown-ups that only yesterday, they professed surprise and joy at learning so much about each other during the first two hours of the training, how much easier it was to talk about themselves when the questions were assigned in addition to the seats, how helpful that their "teachers" explained specific instructions for the speaking order at each table as well as the importance of listening and turn taking. We remind them that good intentions do not make for good conversation; good questions, good facilitation and good rules do! They are equipped with the skills necessary to create a cooperative, connected environment in the classroom under their supervision.

But they must also remember, as professional adults in our classroom, they needed to receive step-by-step guidance from an authority figure in order to ease into the unfamiliar. This is also true for their young students. We offer a quote from this informative book written by Gloria Ladson-Billings:

The Dream Keepers: Successful Teachers of African American Children:

"Affirming identity is not just about being nice---it is about being knowledgeable about who our students are, and reflecting a story that resonates with their best hope for themselves."

The way to affirm the identity of our students is to know and accept them; a classroom teacher quoted in the book, Mary Ginley, explains the downside of "nice":

"A warm friendly teacher is nice but isn't enough. We have plenty of warm and friendly teachers who tell the kids nicely to ask mommy and daddy to speak to them in English at home; who give them easier tasks so they won't feel bad when the work becomes difficult; who never learn what life is like for them at home or what stories they have been told or what their history is."

True acceptance builds trust; trust builds respect; respect builds community. Acceptance allows the teacher to embrace acculturation; acculturation is the best vehicle for encouraging the child to fully absorb an important truth; getting "good" grades and speaking "good" English are not signs of "selling-out." Acculturation gives all of us the ability to add on, without needing to subtract, those things that aren't commonly valued in stereotypical middle class American society. It is what brings a richness of knowledge to the table.

When a teacher decides to choose the members of a classroom work group, assign field trip partners and give them a task to complete together, provides the class with specific, non-intrusive questions for a "get to know you" exercise (samples in the tools section), rather than asking students to commence with ones of the typical and anxiety producing, "Talk about yourselves" variety; they are taking steps to build the foundation for a community of inclusion and acceptance. Tasks lead to talk. Talking gives other people a name and a face. We need not pretend to enjoy everyone with a name and a face, but it's kind of hard to hate them, isn't it?

STEPS FOR THE REST OF US

Hopefully, we have presented sufficient evidence for the need to, and the ability of, an informed classroom teacher to create an environment of acceptance that does not denigrate the individual identity of others within his or her sphere of influence. The classroom is a place uniquely equipped to create community when it is well run. This is a captive audience seeing each other daily, which share an adult mentor and a familiar setting.

Most people do not have the luxury of classroom like proximity to each other, nor the presence of a person charged with facilitating and mediating misunderstandings. Can our bits of advice help those of you hoping to conquer the fear of judgment, anger, or insecurity, flashing through your mind during an uncomfortable encounter with difference experienced in the rush of daily life?

For starters, we feel reasonably assured you will not ask a white woman holding a black child: "Are you the real mother?" The next time you are at a park and see a Latin "looking" woman with a white "looking" baby, you won't quietly pull her aside to ask her if she is interested in a new nanny opportunity with your family, nor will you ask your kid's white friend if they live in a big house with a pool because you think all white people live that way. We are certain anybody reading this book will think twice before declaring: "We are all the same", "I don't see color" or "In America, all of us are treated the same" while speaking to a person of color, and then express feelings of confusion or anger, when the person doesn't agree! For the reader who has paid particularly close attention to our narrative, you will remember to ask questions with an "ask", not with a "tell" dressed in an "ask" disguise; you will likely listen with empathy and seek better understanding. These changes, if accomplished, indicate you have taken significant steps on the road to accessible and honest communication between cultural groups! Yet, friendship takes more.

Look again at the quotes we cited at the start of the chapter "Opening the Doors." Dr. King reminds us of the need for sustained interpersonal relations to get to a place of "knowing"; Attorney general Holder reminds us that our fear of discomfort keeps us a "nation of cowards in matters of race." One hundred years of great American visionaries' coaxing and commanding us to take risks, have moved us only slightly forward in friendship.

We do find solace as we read and digest the following explanation for this difficulty in finding cross-cultural social connection, in the words of Deborah Plummer, author of the book *Racing Across the Lines*:

"Building inclusive work environments is synonymous with managing diversity. Yet you can't give what you don't have. It is a difficult task. Anyone would be at a loss to know how to be inclusive if his or her entire life were singularly focused on same-race experiences."

We understand this to mean that our "cowardice" is to be expected in light of our personal histories, but also have confidence that creating real change in the cross cultural social dynamic of our lives is not nearly as difficult as some of us have come to believe.

First, it is imperative to begin establishing comfortable conversation with adults using the same approach most tend to use with children. Consider these "grown-ups" to be social novices, possessing abundant curiosity, little skill, lots of emotion, and sorely in need of clear, kind, and patient guidance from another with more knowledge and experience! Unfortunately, in the workplaces, cocktail parties and school fundraisers of our lives, we are expected to mingle exactly as we would with other "grown-ups" we greet while attending a neighborhood or family event teaming with folks who share a similar ethnic, age, marital, parental and financial status to our own. These "grown-up" experiences prove the perfect preparation for anybody attending that big office party or fundraiser with hopes of engaging in laughter, dance and cocktail fun with new friends, right? Of course, we are prepared; just be certain to head straight for the table filled with the people who "look like you!"

How differently would the "vibe" in the room feel if suddenly the myriad of social, school, and work events we attended, were hosted by people treating us as if we were young children? We are imagining our host would have created a seating plan in anticipation of that lonely child wandering around pulling nervously at his shirt because he doesn't know where to sit. We envision arriving to a cheerful and welcoming place. We see a room with a few tables; one of them is filled with tasty snacks, another with crafts or paint supplies. Finally, we would expect some sort of entertainment. The entertainment may be a game and a piñata, maybe it involves some singing and dancing to fun music, or even a rowdy balloon-popping contest. It could be the kind with magicians, Disney princesses, face painting and a petting zoo if the host is interested in spending lots of money. Costly or not, kids parties end the same way, with a cake and a group sing. Oh yeah; the party doesn't go on forever either! In fact, the ideal child guest never stays long enough to get mean or cranky. Come to think of it, not bad advice for adult parties either!

Maybe these suggestions sound "tongue in cheek, they aren't. We know these tips are easily translated into the "grown-up" world, and that they work well with a bit of planning. Our strategy is centered on creating an atmosphere of deliberate activity, much like the scene regularly found at a young child's birthday celebration.

We favor icebreakers for a dependable start. An icebreaker need not be one of those elaborately staged "trust walks" reserved for team building seminars at large companies and "hip" tech start-ups. A good one ought to create a memorable moment, with multiple people, in a short period of time. Remember, nobody wants to be stuck in an "engineered" conversation with an unappealing person any more than they want to be stuck in an unappealing spontaneous conversation from which they cannot escape. Your guests will find the ones with whom they shared a positive memorable moment, and want to continue to talk with, later on in the evening. And, like at the children's party, activities change every so often. The kid host knows when it's time for the "next thing", so will you! Trust your eyes, ears and instincts.

One of our favorite conversation starters is called "Wheel in a Wheel". It is the most effective way to get all of your guests into one place, engaging in a "moment" with other guests, while maintaining the ability to speak as deeply or as casually as is comfortable for them. You will need at least fifteen participants, but there is no upper limit. Everyone forms a circle and counts off by two. All of the "ones" take a step inside the circle before turning to face the "two" across from them. The host will pose a question that can be answered by describing a personal experience. Those facing each other will talk together before the host calls time and asks each to step to their right; now all are facing someone new. The host may offer different topics for each pairing or can choose to repeat select questions in order that each participant gains perspective from a new partner.

Questions are designed to be universal and without controversy. This activity can be utilized with any age group and any sort of community by constructing questions tailored to a particular community or situation.

These are a few examples of the general type:

1. Tell your partner about your favorite elementary school teacher.

2. Describe a perfect day. Where are you? What is the setting? What is the activity? Are you alone?

3. What was your worst injury?

4. Talk about something nice a friend did for you.

5. How would friends describe you? Strangers?

6. What is something you wish you learned to do?

7. What is your least favored personality trait in others? What trait do you most admire?

8. Can you describe an experience that left you feeling powerful and brave?

9. Did you ever break a bad habit?

These are some we use with parent groups at schools:

1. Tell your partner a story about something funny your kid did as a toddler.

2. In what ways is your child most like you? In what ways are they different?

3. What do you miss most about having a baby, a toddler etc...? What do you miss least?

4. If you had to pick a trait you favor most in your child's demeanor, which would it be and why?

5. Can you recall an incident in which your child showed a surprising amount of wisdom?

6. Can you talk about a time when your child deliberately separated from you as if they were embarrassed? How did it feel?

7. What about this school most benefits your child? What has been a challenge?

The parent "wheel" questions are often the ones we *wish* we got the chance to discuss with other parents, but instead tread lightly with the "acceptable" and safe variety. Maybe you are reciting them in your head right now even before reading them! "Where do you live? What do you do? What does your husband/wife do? (They seem to forget to use the word partner!), How are your child's teachers? Where does your family go during school break?" For us, these surface "polite" questions are largely designed to sort and compare our status in the social hierarchy. For La Fonda, it's the husband questions that feel most uncomfortable; for Kari, it's the inquiries about the skills, accomplishments, and future plans of her daughter. Not only do these conversations cause discomfort; they become boring and redundant. It's a shame! We attend many of these school orientation meetings, new family dinners and fundraising extravaganzas painstakingly planned and put together with great expense and effort. The organizers go forward with the best intentions of creating an atmosphere that provides all attendees with a sense of community, with the feeling that they are wanted and welcomed. Yet, we tend to use these gatherings as a way to "catch up" with buddies from our neighborhood Starbucks or gym class, or as a way to meet the people we *spotted* at the Starbucks or gym class, the ones we *want* to have as our new buddies, but haven't had the guts to approach!

Our focus on the necessity of facilitating and proctoring a simple meet and mingle gathering in the style of a diversity class, is actually grounded in sound scientific research! The respected sociologist and provost of Columbia University, Claude M. Steele, shares fascinating information in his book, *Whistling Vivaldi*, describing the effect of something he calls "stereotype threat" on our ability to open up to certain people. He presents this exhausting list of locations that may evoke stereotype threat for an individual, a feeling best described as an internal alarm saying, "I have this sense that I will be judged and stereotyped in this situation":

"It is identity threat that keeps people apart and uncomfortable with each other, that prevents passengers from sitting next to each other on airplanes, that discourages students from taking courses with substantial numbers of minority students in them, or that may make teachers reluctant to approach some minority students."

Professor Steele wanted to study the phenomenon; he hoped to help the participants in his "racial profiling" research to speak more freely with each other:

"We tried first to assure them that they wouldn't be judged by what they said in the conversation, that they should feel free to speak their minds without fear of recrimination. It didn't work. Perhaps they didn't believe us. Those who anticipated talking to black partners about racial profiling sat father away from each other. Next, we assured them that the differences in perspective were valued, that a range of perspectives was appreciated in these conversations. This didn't work either. These strategies seemed reasonable to us. We'd gotten from a diversity workshop we'd seen. They had an unforeseen consequence: the more we assured the group that we wouldn't hold their words against them, the more they feared we would. It's difficult to assure away the stereotype threat whites can feel in interracial situations, or anyone can feel in situations where negative stereotypes about them feel relevant. Stereotypes about our identities hover in the air around us. If we are invested in what we're doing, we get worried; we try to disprove the stereotype. We avoid situations where we have to contend with this pressure."

Instead of spouting out hollow assurances, he found greater success utilizing the *"mindset"* message he learned from the author and professor, Carol Dweck. She suggests focusing on a belief or "mindset" that the goal of the conversation is simply to learn from each other. He explains the rational:

"When interactions between people from different backgrounds have learning from each other as a goal, it eases the potential tension between them, giving missteps less significance. Trust is fostered"

At the start of our diversity training, we mention learning as the primary goal. We also tell the class, "Bias is normal; if you don't feel bias, you are not thinking." Usually the announcement is met with audible gasps! "Our goal is to teach you how to recognize bias in yourselves and to help you to start exploring the roots and meanings of these feelings in your daily life. All will likely gain a better understanding of these sometimes embarrassing, but completely normal thoughts, if we look back at, observe the exteriors of, and search deep within, our past and current lives with curiosity and truth."

Translation: *"TRUST US AND JUMP IN"* Jumping in doesn't work so well if the facilitator doesn't jump in first! The admission of our own bias is imperative in our opinion. We pull out a few examples we think are worth sharing with the group. Kari might tell the story about going camping with a bunch of friends who decided to ask each other stuff from the personally intimate *"Book of Questions" by Edmond Jabes for* an evening activity around the campfire. The person to whom the question is addressed must answer immediately and with the first thing that pops into his or her head. Kari is asked, "When you see a woman with big fancy sunglasses drive past you in a Cadillac Escalade, your first thought is…" "Who's her husband?" is her quick answer. Kari then realizes this is sexist. She wonders why it did not occur to her that this woman might have made her own money. Shawn may talk about the time in a checkout line at a CVS when he "knew for sure" that the white guy who cut in front of him did it because Shawn is black. He was about to give "that racist a piece of my mind" when the man turned around, saw Shawn, and blurted out "I am so sorry, sir, I didn't see you there."

We might follow our "confessions" by sharing evidence of the prevalence of unconscious bias culled from a variety of books and academic journal articles by sociologists and anthropologists utilizing stringent university research methods.

One of the narratives comes from the book "Whistling Vivaldi", as told by the author, Claude Steele. He describes the difficulty he had getting open responses from college students tasked with having a discussion about racial profiling as part of his research. They were not comfortable opening up. He ended up with more and better responses when he began the orientation by telling participants their task was to learn from each other's stories. This was not a political discussion. This was not about who is right or wrong; it was simply a learning opportunity. We have found that by adding our own, often embarrassing, "learning experiences" to Dr. Steel's helpful rules for discussion, we set a tone for a more open and a less "guarded" engagement by students.

Admittedly, our suggestions for getting more conversational substance from your acquaintances and colleagues could be daunting. The idea of hosting a completely *"orchestrated"* party, or presiding over rounds of our "wheel in a wheel" activity, may cause you to break out in a sweat. If this is the case, you are not alone! In fact, in addition to attending classes, our students are assigned "homework" we developed in order to encourage them to engage their world with more awareness and curiosity than they had previously. This "homework" could prove an excellent start for anyone.

One of the assignments is called the "Eyes Open Journal." We came up with the idea for this journal after reading the book *"Blink"* by Malcolm Gladwell. In the book, Gladwell provides the reader with fascinating instance after fascinating instance of ways in which our first fleeting sight of something, or of someone, brings forth biased opinions and actions of which we are completely unaware. Some of the "blink" stories recounted in Gladwell's book, have proved fleeting bias to be deadly, others, that it is disconcerting, and some that are just plain amazing! This country has recently witnessed a seeming never ending series of tragic deaths resulting from internal race bias on the part of police officers. Sadly, studies have proved this bias to be a problem for years. One experiment cited in the book illustrating deadly bias, requires police officers to observe split second flashes of photos depicting single men holding soda cans, wallets or guns. They are told they will be tested on their reaction time while deciding whether the man in the photo is armed or not. Some of the men pictured are black and some are white. The black men are "shot" more quickly than the white men most of the time. This is because an officer will wait that crucial moment longer to see what is in the hand of the white "offender".

We found the Implicit Bias test to be the most disconcerting. In this "test", computer images of all sorts of people are quickly flashed across the screen. At the same time, the screen flashes descriptive words such as nice, smart, poor, or compassionate. The test subjected is assessed on the speed with which they assign the word to the image of a person. Test takers will assign "positive" traits more quickly to whites depicted in the photos. Black test takers will also show some bias towards blacks. We are fans of the IBT because it measures all sorts of bias. One can explore a slew of their own biases in regard to their views on the age, gender, sexual orientation or beauty of the face on the screen. The test is private and readily available to anyone with access to a computer screen and keyboard. Give it a try!

Finally, the *Blink* chapter we felt was just plain amazing, allowed the test subject to spend fifteen minutes alone in the dorm room of another student whom he or she does not know and will not meet. They must describe the individual who lives in the room based only on what objects are seen. The descriptions of the personality of the unknown occupant are surprisingly accurate.

We hoped that by sharing examples of the obvious bias "normal everyday" folks like us experience, we would encourage students to approach their *"Open Eyes Journal"* assignment with honesty and a sense of curiosity. Most times, the results are filled with both. It can be strange and exhausting to pay close attention to the fleeting "Blink" thoughts bombarding your brain for the unfiltered journaling portion of the task, but do it with gusto before looking back to consider and process the meaning of a particular "flash" for you. We check in with each other to compare "flashes" now and then. We had quite an enlightening talk about choosing physicians from the health insurance directory. Kari starts with zip code since she hates to drive. Fonda starts with recommendations from friends and family. Both skip over names they can't pronounce. Kari moves on to "college attended" and then, names that don't sound Jewish. Fonda has preference for the "Jewish" names both for doctors and for accountants. Kari says she doesn't look for "Jewish" names because of a bias that they are "probably full of themselves" and don't feel the need to try hard. Fonda admits a bias that Beverly Hills and Jewish are synonymous with "good" when it comes to choosing a Doctor or an Accountant. How about you?

Listen to your flashes of dislike, preference or confusion while driving, watching television or walking through a shop. Are you more likely to show anger to a male or female driver, to one driving an expensive or economy car, or to a driver of a different ethnic group? Are you more judgmental towards people who look like you, or the ones more obviously from another ethnic, age or income group. The information is enlightening. We learn so much from them that we challenge other friends to join us by jotting down meaningful flashes of their own.

Our friend and co-trainer, Shawn, gave us his notes from two particularly powerful experiences and graciously allowed us to share them with you. The first is a stream of conscience kind of mantra that went through his mind as he stood around his office casually speaking with a group of white co-workers:

"Just don't screw up and use the word "be"; if you use the word in a sentence, you might slip up and say something like "He be, "They be" or "It be" by mistake. They will think you are stupid. They will think you can't speak proper English. Better to avoid "Be" altogether.

The second was written to us in a letter:

Dear Kari and La Fonda,
   "So Neilsen had a goodbye party for an employee at an executive's house in the Sunset Hills. I thought it would be good for my career to attend and get to know some executives. During the party one of the exec's came over to the group of people I was with and turned to me and introduced herself. She asked if I was there with Cindi, the only other Black person there. I said "No, I'm not with her." I told her I was a supervisor and had met her before at one of the town hall meetings. She was gracious and apologetic. She said she saw us speak earlier. I told her I understood there are a thousand employees at Neilsen. Previously, I would have been fit to be tied that she assumed we were a couple because we were both black. As you know, I have self esteem issues that really bubble to the top when at a party with a majority of whites. I automatically think they think less of me, which makes me want to get power through anger.
After talking to you guys, I a better able to stay calm and question the situation. You taught me to think about

*the attitude of the person, that they might be dumb to
their words. I try to think more about teachable moments
instead of just getting angry. I am more able to maintain
that calmness because when I walk into a room of high
faluten white people I just think to myself, maybe there
is a Kari Bower in the room, relax and go find her."*

We had lunch with another friend recently. He told us
he was trying to practice being more aware of "little
things" and his reactions to them after hearing about our
book. He asked us if we thought it "was weird" that he was
bothered when office mates decided the punishment for
whomever finished the office fantasy football pool in last
place had to wear a Micheal Samm jersey all day. We did
not think it was weird at all. We assured our friend that
we thought it incredibly offensive to believe that wearing
the shirt of a gay male athlete is only for "losers!"

With practice, this self-conscious journaling method
flows easily, and yes, on occasion, can be tough to shut
off! For instance, Kari thought she might be getting "too
obsessed" when she shared this conversation:

"I was walking through the park with a long time friend
after a fun night listening to music on the lawn at the
County museum. We passed by one of those big fuzzy German
Shepherds. In the middle of talking about something else,
I announced, "That looks like a Nazi dog" The white man
from North Carolina ponders this for a moment, then
replies, "No, that dog screams Selma to me!"

Perhaps, a less mentally strenuous, but still
interesting and eye opening experience, sounds better to

you. We offer another option to our classes. This one is called immersion and reflection. Participants must spend at least a few hours in a location in which they are a visibly noticeable minority and interact with the majority population. They may choose to shop, eat or just walk around in another ethnic neighborhood or attend an unfamiliar religious or social event. However, do not venture out with more than one other person. Groups tend to focus inward and loose the possibility of interaction with local residents. With luck, time, and the right amount of "feeling "out of place", we hope the experience will provide a taste of minority life. Be sure to "feel" with your entire body; feel your heart beat, feel yourself walk less confidently, feel your face get hot when the passerby doesn't smile at you like "normal"

Maybe you aren't the adventurous type, or maybe you don't live near areas known to be densely populated with people who look, sound and live differently from yourself; we have a third option. It's not the best method, but it is not at all useless; sit back on the couch and absorb some of that ubiquitous media. We have conducted plenty of research for this book sitting back, eating snacks and watching a big flat screen! We have been known to hit the pause button, smoke cigarettes, advise each other on everything from kids to clothes, and then come back around to the content of whatever we happen to be watching. Not surprisingly, this couch time has gotten us into some of our best conversations!

Of course, content is the operative word here. So much of what we see and hear hits us in a traumatic flash. The broadcast news outlets and major newspapers feed us a constant diet of violent, scary and sad results. We see no *before* in the lives of Michael Brown or Eric Garner. There is no readily available context. It was months after Michael Brown died on the pavement, months after the acquittal of Wilson, before we heard anything about cause.

Only the few who committed themselves to watching an endless loop of death, fire and unruly anger for weeks on end, heard the bigger, but much quieter, story from Ferguson, the story of the methodical and unrelenting ticketing, fining and jailing of it's black residents by the local police force. Yes, without a doubt, we need to see the hash reality of the blood, the fire and the tears. Cell phone video has become an immeasurable gift for a disbelieving, financially secure, geographically distant, and largely white community, but it isn't the whole story. In fact, seeing, hearing and reading *only* the horror, can have a devastating effect on the folks most directly affected by the horror. Consider these words of wisdom spoken by the artist, author and professor, Nell Irvin Painter, while addressing the audience during the lecture "Race In America" at the 2015 Harlem book festival:

"This constant barrage of atrocities is psychologically traumatizing. It feels almost like a conspiracy to keep us from our work. As a historian, I don't feel there are more black people being murdered just that we are hearing about it more. In a very sad and perverse way, that's a step forward, but speaking psychologically, we have to find means for coming to terms with the atrocities. It could mean going to the streets, joining organizations, giving money. We have to be able to take steps, because to do Something gives you some space and lets you then continue with your own work."

In fact, a bit of anecdotal evidence indicates that Media outlets in other countries aren't "All atrocity all the time!" Kari was in London for three days this past June and returned with a copy of the June 16 London Times. One plain old Tuesday morning drinking coffee and reading the mainstream newspaper left at the hotel room door…

JUST ONE DAY AND FOUR DIFFERENT COVER STORIES DESCRIBING A VARIETY OF WAYS IN WHICH AVERAGE BRITISH CITIZENS ARE QUIETLY DISADVANTAGED IN THE JOB MARKET DUE TO THEIR REGIONAL ACCENT, ADDRESS, ATTENDANCE AT A UNIVERSITY NOT DEEMED ELITE ENOUGH, A LIMITED TRAVEL RESUME OR LACK OF SOCIAL CONNECTION!

Tales of common micro-aggressions well illustrated, explained, and discussed in black and white, Amazing!

These are not the race and class stories we see on the front page of a mainstream paper in the U.S. Instead, when our media is providing information about race and class, it is centered on the heartless cop or the damaged terrorist criminal killing unarmed people in the street; it is about brown people invading our borders; it's about a crazy white lady drowning her five young children because "The lord told her to". We read and watch stories that have us shaking our heads in sadness and shock while we smugly tell ourselves:

"I would never shoot anyone, how disgusting; I am not a racist, Why weren't the authorities told about that religious nutcase in Texas? I see everyone as equal; I am a good person!"

How would it feel for the CEO's and employers in our lives and in our cities, to drink their morning coffee while reading this paragraph from the Times London? :

"Too many banks, law firms and accountants are hiring in their own image, drawing from a narrow pool and wasting the talent of a generation! Top companies are hiring too many of the privately educated Oxbridge graduates with the "right" accents while excluding bright working class candidates." The chairman of the headmasters and headmistresses association disagreed, arguing, "Pupils won places at the best Universities because of hard work and intelligence. It is unfair to put a barrier in front of young people who gained a place through sheer work and call that a posh test. It is a skills test!"

We imagine the internal feeling would be more than a simple, "What a disgusting racist." These stories and opinions are more complex and difficult to dismiss. Maybe, they cause the reader to spend a bit more time considering their own hiring preferences and practices? Who knows, it's possible! At least he or she may feel themselves part of the situation, not only a concerned and confused outside observer.

It's true, much American media does deliver a preponderance of the "If it bleeds, it leads" sort of content, but we also found a nice amount of quality, thought provoking stuff. No excuses! We urge you to watch the news hour and frontline on PBS, Super Soul Sunday and Our America with Lisa Ling. Check out the reality shows I am Jazz, I am Cait or The Little Couple for helpful insight into lives we rarely experience. The documentaries 'Good Hair" and "Dark Girls" offer much about the lives of black girls from many perspectives. MTV developed and broadcast the documentary "White People" in which the documentarian, Jose Vargas, travels to a few different American communities and briefly explores the meaning of whiteness for the white people he interviews. Certainly, the Netflix or HBO documentary libraries contain hours of eye popping, brain feeding and soul nourishing programming. Book TV on CSPAN is full of panel discussions and interviews with non-fiction authors, many discussing race, class and american history. Often, we find these interviews more valuable than the books themselves. For those who look to their portable screens far more than television check out the Critical Media Project designed by faculty and students from the Annenberg School of Communications at USC. It's full of thought provoking video and commentary centered on the cultural stereotypes we are constantly exposed to in our media consuming life and the effect these messages have on our thoughts and behavior. Are you in the mood for a sitcom? Some of the most thought provoking shows about American culture are the comedies created by Norman Lear and broadcast in the 1970's. Fortunately, our digital age has made viewing these groundbreakers simple. Believe it or not, Keeping Up with the Kardashians was not the first show to air conversations about gender identity issues. Norman Lear told a journalist that his favorite episode of All In the Family was one about a transgender woman. The shows All in The Family, Maude, The Jefferson's and Good Times, wrap copious amounts of information, depth and soul into a VERY FUNNY package.

If we would have attempted to develop a list of culturally relevant situation comedies even two years back, the list would have included mostly 1970s' greats, jumped ahead to the 90's to add "The Bernie Mac Show" and "In Living Color", skipped 10 more years before recommending our favorite, Everybody Hates Chris, and well, ending there. We are happy to recommend a couple of new ones to watch. We laugh and learn in equal amounts watching either Fresh Off the Boat or Blackish; both of these sitcoms center around stable middle class families living in majority white communities and workplaces, while hilariously and honestly navigating issues of race, culture, and family in each episode.

The writing and the immersing, the reading and the watching; all are legitimate vehicles for improving our awareness and understanding of other peoples lives. Alertness and awareness make for a good foundation. Increasing awareness is especially needed for members of the white community who are rarely, if ever, required to navigate cultural difference. Our personal foundation is solid enough to have added the walls, windows and doors called friendship. These scattered "houses" of culturally mixed friendships and families are few, but growing every day. In fact, our experience has shown us, that what seems to be growing faster than the houses themselves, is the desire to build more of them.

We were surprised on a Sunday in July to see a new and different "race" story covered on the morning network news. Both ABC and CNN decided to break from their endless expert discussion on the intersection of race, police brutality, violence and poverty, and run stories about the possibility of positive connection between culturally different communities. On ABC, the news show, "This week with George Stephanopolis", broadcast a segment about an art installation meant to connect strangers around the world in conversation. The "art" piece is actually a shipping container the size of a small room, painted gold and fitted with a skype screen. One enters the "box" prepared to converse with the stranger on the screen "live" from somewhere in Iran, Afghanistan or Cuba. A participant has no idea who is "inside"; not the age, gender, ethnicity, religion or sexual orientation of the other. It turns out this installation got an entire segment on the Sunday news because it is VERY popular! People got permission to ask or answer anything to a total stranger and actually want to wait in line to do it.

The CNN Sunday show, "Fareed Zacharia GPS", aired a segment about social engineering in Singapore. The host explained that all housing and schools in Singapore are required by law to be integrated by people of all backgrounds and income levels. Yes, Singapore, the self-described nanny state, uses "quotas" to determine who lives in every building in every neighborhood. Mr. Zacharia then provokes viewers by staring into the camera, and suggesting: "They may have got it right"

Finally, we enjoyed one of those great Oprah "ah-hah moments" while listening to the writer Patricia Hill Collins speak these words as she greeted a crowd of students assembled to listen to her talk at a Washington D.C. café called Busboys and Poets:

"Thank you for inviting me today. In our world, it is difficult to find a space to share ideas. This is that sort of space"

Now, for the "ah-hah" part; Dr. Collins first talked to her audience about the *space*! Indeed, it is unique in comparison to a typical lecture hall or a room lined with rows of metal chairs, where the majority of these talks happen. Busboys and Poets is dimly lit, has big round tables placed in front of cushioned booths and smaller round tables in the center. Coffee, tea and snacks are served. *A second "ah-hah" follows*; should a comfortable and inclusive gathering space be so rare that a seasoned poet marvels at its very existence? We looked at the website. In addition to the menu and event listings, the

Busboys and Poets website posts a paragraph called a tribal statement:

Busboys and Poets is a community where racial and cultural connections are consciously uplifted...a place to take a deliberate pause and feed your mind, body and soul...a space for art, culture and politics to intentionally collide, a place where we can inspire social change and begin to transform our community and the world.

The third and final "ahh-hah" came as a simple question;

Why aren't there more places like this?

Is it naïve to imagine a comfortable coffee shop or restaurant hosting speakers on intriguing topics now and then? Must the few comfortable and affordable venues in town be reserved solely for observation and listening opportunities? Let's add dynamic speakers and dialogue to the calendars of these establishments along with the usual menu of acoustic concerts, open mike nights and poetry slams.

Is it naïve to imagine a Starbucks that provides not only a place to grab a coffee and run, not only a place to open your laptop in silence when you aren't running, but instead, a place that occasionally becomes an interactive destination? Mr. Shultz, we really admire the heart and soul you put into the "Race Together" effort. Engaging other hearts and souls is a tough job for anyone, often requiring huge amounts of focus, time and trust. Maybe there is a way to add more of these elements to your community building efforts. Why not alert patrons in advance that your store will host a two-hour evening event now and then. Possibly, the event is centered on an interesting current topic and facilitated by a featured speaker? We brainstormed the idea! It would be free, open to all, and the food and beverage could be half price for an extra incentive. We envision this type of pre-planned destination experience to be highly likely to attract the more willing learners among your customers and then naturally expand over time by word of mouth.

Willing learners are good listeners. Good listening is difficult. The author Malcolm Gladwell, who has made an enviable career writing some of the most fascinating books about human behavior ever written, says his best interviews are the ones where he barely spoke. He called "good listening" "exhausting" during a lecture at the 92nd street Y in New York City. As he explained the silent exhaustion of good listening, his co-lecturer nodded his head excitedly in agreement. Gladwell shared the stage with Brian Grazer, the iconic film producer and author of the bestselling 2015 book, A Curious Mind: The Secret to a Bigger Life. Grazer's book is a collection of thirty years worth of "curiosity conversations" with a wide range of experts on a litany of subjects. He added the following to Gladwell's remarks on the importance of showing your subject they are being heard:

"I definitely agree! You feel the energy that the person is connecting to you because they can feel the energy from you that you are very alert."

Ask yourself what this "alert listening energy" feels like; ask yourself what it looks and sounds like when the face across the table from you is alert…and then, when it isn't! We bet you can describe it easily, as can we! The face is not looking away or around, it doesn't look like it is anxiously trying to open it's mouth the moment you breath, and it doesn't say "I understand" without adding a question or comment demonstrating true interest. Lets face it; we all know the difference because we have been at the table. Sometimes we are the bored or interruptive party and sometimes it's the other/s. Poor listening behavior is normal, common, and sometimes even justified; just know it is always detected. Us humans can fake all kinds of stuff; listening well is definitely not one of them. Brian Grazer and Malcolm Gladwell are seasoned professionals. They know how to listen, extract what is important and then retell and rework the best stuff for the reader. They begin the process with sincere and obvious curiosity. We understand and accept that all people are not curious. We have seen plenty of evidence supporting the upside for the age-old assertion, "ignorance is bliss." Although, we do have a hard time accepting the folks who insist, "I am curious, I really want to hear about it" right before jumping into a monologue of "tells" followed by question marks. You remember we taught you about those pesky "dressed up" questions that are really statements and opinions. For example, "How can you possibly drive that far every day?" or "Haven't you heard day care can be dangerous? Do you really need to go back to work?" "Were your child's grade good enough for that school or did he/she get in because of affirmative action?" or "You look mixed, what are you?" , "Were you upset when you knew you couldn't have you own children?", "Are you afraid to live in that neighborhood?" If you are truly curious, be vigilant when choosing the words and tone of your "innocent" questions, the ones that seem to somehow "inexplicably" offend another who is just "way too sensitive". By the way, remember that listening involves your body language too!

Conclusion

Is it possible to truly walk our talk? That all depends on your definition of walking ones talk. If your definition is that "people are people and I treat everyone equally" or "We are all the same inside", we would say walking your talk is likely impossible. However, if you define the phrase as we do; walking your talk is being vigilantly self aware of your thoughts, words and actions before and during an interaction, then you are "getting it" and are on the right track. We believe that walking our talk means we can sense what attracts, repels, mystifies, scares, interests or inspires us, and we understand or want to figure out *why* this occurs. There is something about figuring the why of our thoughts and words that helps us remove the "edge" or imbalance we feel when around folks who repel or confuse us. We learn how to mentally shift a bit and engage kindly and simply with the offender in our midst.

Walking our talk doesn't require like; it requires acceptance. Our talk tells us to be as aware, authentic and respectful as possible. It takes practice to learn to get away from the repellant without conflict and more comfortably approach and engage the interesting, but distant, people within our zone of possible contact. Take your time. In fact, more important than that, put down your phone, lift your eyes and don a kind of half smile while walking through those grocery isles, coffee shops, public parks and subway trains in your life. *There exists an opening for conversation only when you give off an "open" vibe.* You will be disappointed at times. Maybe you will be disappointed in yourself for failing to "say the right thing" or feel badly towards another person for their behavior now and then. The rewards beat the risk.

Witnessing another person engage in the act of empathetic and attentive listening without any need or obligation to do so, and without the knowledge that anyone is watching, is to witness a magical moment of humanity. We saw such a moment during the film "Ghetto Physics". Cornel West, one of our countries most vocal advocates of the importance of empathy, was unknowingly being filmed with a cell phone camera as he was hurrying across the street with the films director, having what seemed an animated discussion. A couple of cameramen trailed behind, cameras pointing down at the ground and turned off. A disheveled looking man approached the group yelling "Hey Cornel" a couple of times. The picture is grainy and distant; the sound is muffled but intelligible. We held our breath, each silently begging in our head, "Please don't let this towering elite act elitist! Our Dr. West did not disappoint; he reacted to this loud and intrusive fellow with kindness, curiosity and good listening; the scene unfolds:

Dr. West stands still, steps out from the protection of his circling friends and gives his hand to the man asking, "How are you brother?" with trademark enthusiasm. The man answers; "I wanted to say hello to you man, and show you my painting." Dr. West takes the painting slowly, holds it in front of him with both hands, looks it over carefully and declares; "Brother, you are a true artist! I would like to buy this beautiful painting if you are willing to sell it to me."

The man is elated, his mouth open in awe. Cornel West removes a wad of large bills from his pocket and gives the artist what appears to be hundreds of dollars; the money handed in such a matter of fact and sweet way, nobody watching would suspect pity or charity had a part in this exchange. We learned a lesson in patience and humility in those moments. We hope it is a lesson never forgotten!

Barkley, Charles, and Michael Wilbon. *Who's Afraid of a Large Black Man?* New York: Penguin, 2005. Print.

Bennett, Rosemary. "Bosses under Fire for Hiring Staff Who Are Just like Them." *The Times of London* 16 June 2015: 17. Print.

Bernard, Emily. *Some of My Best Friends: Writings on Interracial Friendships*. New York: Amistad, 2004. Print.

Blow, Charles M. "The Obamas, Race and Slights." *The New York Times*. The New York Times, 17 Dec. 2014. Web. 6 Sept. 2015.

Bronson, Po, and Ashley Merryman. *NurtureShock: New Thinking about Children*. New York: Twelve, 2009. Print.

Chang, Jeff. *Who We Be: The Colorization of America*. N.p.: St. Martin's, 2014. Print.

Coates, Ta-Nehisi. Between the World and Me. Spiegel & Grau, *July 2015.* Print

Crossfire Magazine [Santa Monica] Mar. 2013, March 2013 ed., Op Ed sec.: 39. Print.

Deresiewicz, William. "The Disadvantages of an Elite Education." *The American Scholar:*. N.p., Summer 2008. Web.

DeSteno, David. "The Science of Compassion." N.p., 14 July 2012. Web.

DiAngelo, Robin. "White Fragility." *The International Journal of Critical Pedagogy* 3.3 (2011): n. pag. *The International Journal of Critical Pedagogy*. 2011. Web.

DiTomaso, Nancy. *The American Non-dilemma: Racial Inequality without Racism*. N.p.: Russell Sage Foundation, 2012. Print.

Friedman, Devin. "Will You Be My Black Friend?" *GQ*. N.p., Nov. 2009. Web. 06 Sept. 2015.

Gladwell, Malcolm. *Blink: The Power of Thinking without Thinking*. New York: Little, Brown, 2005. Print.

Graham, Lawrence Otis. "I Taught My Black Kids That Their Elite Upbringing Would Protect Them from Discrimination. I Was Wrong." *Washington Post*. The Washington Post, 6 Nov. 2014. Web.

Grazer, Brian. *A Curious Mind: The Secret to a Bigger Life*. New York: Simon and Schuster, 2015. Print

Harris-Perry, Melissa V. *Sister Citizen: Shame, Stereotypes, and Black Women in America*. New Haven: Yale UP, 2011. Print.

Hobbs, Jeff. *The Short and Tragic Life of Robert Peace: A Brilliant Young Man Who Left Newark for the Ivy League*. N.p.: Scribner, 2014. Print.

Huang, Eddie. *Fresh off the Boat: A Memoir*. New York: Spiegel & Grau, 2013. Print.

Joshi, Nirmal. "Doctor, Shut Up and Listen." *The New York Times*. N.p., 4 Jan. 2015. Web.

Marx, Patricia. "The World Capital of Plastic Surgery." *The New Yorker* (2015): n. pag. *The New Yorker*. 23 Mar. 2015. Web.

Morin, Monte. "Study of LGBT Attitudes and Surprises." *The Los Angeles Times* 13 Dec. 2014: n. pag. Print.

Myers, Jim. *Afraid of the Dark*. N.p.: Chicago Review, 2001. Print.
Plummer, Deborah L. *Racing across the Lines: Changing Race Relations through Friendship*. Cleveland: Pilgrim, 2004. Print.

Rankine, Claudia. *Citizen: An American Lyric*. N.p.: Graywolf, 2014. Print.

Sotomayor, Sonia. *My Beloved World*. New York: Knopf, 2013. Print.

Steele, Claude. *Whistling Vivaldi: And Other Clues to How Stereotypes Affect Us*. New York: W.W. Norton, 2010. Print.

Tatum, Beverly Daniel. *Can We Talk about Race?: And Other Conversations in an Era of School Resegregation*. Boston, MA: Beacon, 2007. Print.

Taulbert, Clifton L. *The Invitation*. N.p.: New South, 2014. Print.